"In these insightful pages, David ⟨...⟩ .nis-siology for today. While his assumptions are anchored in Scripture, his understanding flows out of his rich global experience as a missionary leader and trainer. His passion for Jesus and his mission are both inspiring and contagious!"

Bob Fetherlin, president, One Mission Society

"David Sills has provided missionaries, students, pastors and Christian leaders with a thoughtful, future-directed look at the trends, opportunities and challenges that all who are serious about the work of global missions must consider. Grounded in an unflinching commitment to the good news of the gospel and the priority of the Great Commission, the skillful analysis found in this volume raises the right questions, explores the key issues and gives us a wise and responsible compass to help guide our way in an ever-changing world. It is a genuine privilege to recommend this relevant, readable and highly engaging book."

David S. Dockery, president, Trinity International University

"There's no one I trust more to mentor me in the practicalities of effective missions than Dr. Sills. In this book, his decades of experience and balanced wisdom help me navigate the hyperbole and overreactions that are so common. This will be a trusted resource I go back to often."

Bill Walsh, director of international outreach, The Gospel Coalition

"The tools and strategies missionaries use to carry out the Great Commission have evolved more in the last two decades than during any other period of history. Though the Commission itself does not change, rapid growth in technology and global interconnectedness has created new challenges that require us to rethink how we engage in local communities. David Sills's timely book recognizes this shifting paradigm, challenges us to adapt and provides the perspective necessary to grow effectively in the twenty-first century."

Bob Creson, president, Wycliffe Bible Translators

"In a world with numerous pressures shaping the church, David Sills has written an excellent work drawing our attention to some of them. *Changing World, Unchanging Mission* calls us to action as kingdom citizens, challenging us to be students of both God's Word and God's world! A must-read for those desiring to reach the nations!"

J. D. Payne, pastor of church multiplication, The Church at Brook Hills, Birmingham, author of *Apostolic Church Planting*

"Does a changing world necessitate a changed mission? No! Quite the opposite. It necessitates changes in missions but not a changed mission. Our changing world stands in desperate need of an unchanging mission—changing missions but not changing mission! This book should be required reading for every short-term missionary and for every aspiring career missionary as well. It is also recommended reading for all who support them with money and prayer."

David J. Hesselgrave, emeritus professor of mission, Trinity Evangelical Divinity School

CHANGING WORLD, UNCHANGING MISSION

RESPONDING TO
GLOBAL CHALLENGES

M. DAVID SILLS

IVP Books

An imprint of InterVarsity Press
Downers Grove, Illinois

InterVarsity Press
P.O. Box 1400, Downers Grove, IL 60515-1426
ivpress.com
email@ivpress.com

InterVarsity Press® is the book-publishing division of InterVarsity Christian Fellowship/USA®, a movement of students and faculty active on campus at hundreds of universities, colleges and schools of nursing in the United States of America, and a member movement of the International Fellowship of Evangelical Students. For information about local and regional activities, visit intervarsity.org.

Scripture quotations, unless otherwise noted, are from The Holy Bible, English Standard Version, copyright © 2001 by Crossway Bibles, a division of Good News Publishers. Used by permission. All rights reserved.

While any stories in this book are true, some names and identifying information may have been changed to protect the privacy of individuals.

Published in association with the literary agency of Wolgemuth & Associates.

Cover design: Cindy Kiple
Interior design: Beth McGill
Images: open Bible: © Kevin Landwer-Johan/iStockphoto
    air travel aerial view: © Harvepino/iStockphoto
    old paper background: © Kontrec/iStockphoto
    Earth: © Kathy Konkle/iStockphoto

ISBN 978-0-8308-4430-2 (print)
ISBN 978-0-8308-9876-3 (digital)

Printed in the United States of America ∞

Library of Congress Cataloging-in-Publication Data

Sills, Michael David, 1957-
    Changing world, unchanging mission : responding to global challenges / M. David Sills.
        pages cm
    Includes bibliographical references and index.
    ISBN 978-0-8308-4430-2 (pbk. : alk. paper)
    1. Missions. 2. Globalization. I. Title.
    BV2061.3.S585 2015
    266--dc23

                                                                        2015018832

P   20   19   18   17   16   15   14   13   12   11   10   9   8   7   6   5   4   3   2   1

Y   31   30   29   28   27   26   25   24   23   22   21   20   19   18   17   16   15

To Emma and Mary Elle,

the newest members of my precious family.

You are both a fresh and constant reminder of the future,

and even though the world is constantly changing,

the Lord helps us meet its challenges by

sending fresh blessings to meet it.

Contents

- 1 -

Competing and
Conflicting Missions

I ARRIVED ON THE MISSION FIELD three months after I graduated from seminary. The Lord had saved me in my mid-twenties and called me to missions shortly afterward. My wife and I embraced that call and went to seminary to prepare for the field. We were appointed as missionaries as soon as I graduated, and when we moved to the field we went with two small children and eager hearts, but very little else. We had virtually no awareness of what a missionary actually does in everyday work. Seminary had given me a general overview of the history and theology of missions, along with some basic knowledge of strategies and methodologies, but on arrival in our country of service the advice of older missionaries sometimes drastically conflicted with what I had learned.

What was even more concerning was that developing world events such as the fall of the Berlin Wall, the proliferation of the Internet and a burgeoning Latin American liberation theology were changing the rules of the game, if not the entire playing field. I realized early on the importance for missionaries to maintain awareness of world developments. I also realized that sweeping world changes could easily carry away those who are enamored with them unless they stay anchored to the Word of God. How could I possibly know how to sort out wise guidance from my missions education, counsel from godly missionaries who had served faithfully in my new country, and still factor in all the changes around me along with those just about to happen? How can you?

While the world changes daily and many global developments are influencing the way the world acts, interacts and reacts, the gospel is the truth once-for-all delivered to the saints. The question at hand is how missionaries can move with the times and embrace the modern realities and innovations while remaining faithful to God's Word.

This book is not another textbook or exhaustive treatment of the history, theology, philosophies, biblical exegesis or strategies of missions. Many basic evangelical positions and missiological assumptions guide my thinking, and I will point out some of them along the way, but I will refrain from indulging in biblical exegesis, rehearsing historical missiology or engaging in theological debate. I simply want to help missions students, new missionaries, career field missionaries and their mission agencies ask and answer these questions: What can we learn from the ways past changes affected missions? What place should the future have in informing the ways we currently do missions?

Multinational corporations highly value the information yielded from well-researched trends and use it to be proactive in product development, marketing and investment strategies. Missionaries and missions agencies must anticipate and prepare for world change just as diligently. Unfortunately, far too often the missions enterprise is more reactive than proactive.

What place does the future have in informing the ways we do missions? Many cultures around the world are crisis oriented while others are not. Those of a crisis orientation tend to look forward and anticipate the future in front of them. Other cultures consider what is in their past to be in front of them. After all, they would say, the only times of your life you can "see" are those that are past; the future is unknown and therefore behind you. Noncrisis cultures tend not to plan for future possibilities, such as purchasing life or health insurance policies, taking out warranties on automobiles, contributing to retirement plans, or saving for a rainy day. They do not consider such potential problems and so do not plan for them.

What does this have to do with understanding the challenges and concerns of missions today? Do you consider the weather forecast when making plans for a fishing trip or a picnic, or would you check forecasts of job markets for employment possibilities when choosing a college major? Many people anticipate and begin planning for their children's college education even when they are still young. Those of us seeking to impact nations for Christ should consider the trends that lead multinational corporations and the world's governments to adjust, redirect and refocus their efforts to influence nations for the coming decades. Often, hardworking and faithful missionaries are so engaged in their work that they fail to see what is going on in the world or what is coming down the road. It has often been said that the faithful pastor should conduct his ministry with a Bible in one hand and a newspaper in the other. Imagine the pastors who continue to minister and preach as they did thirty years ago, with no change in the music or leadership of their churches, or any awareness of either world events or local changes. While God's Word never changes, the world ever changes. To minister effectively, missionaries must engage the world that is, not the world that was. To know how missionaries should adjust for future trends and changes, we must first consider what our unchanging mission is.

WHAT IS THE MISSION OF THE CHURCH?

The world is shrinking. We come into daily contact with more and more diverse people, and this brings an increasing awareness of the needs of the world—gospel needs as well as social, educational, physical and financial needs. In a world as advanced as ours, the reality is that over twenty thousand children die of starvation and hunger-related diseases every day.[1] Two thousand people die from the lack of clean drinking water daily.[2] Diarrhea kills more than four thousand children every day and malaria continues to kill one child every thirty seconds.[3] Thirty-five percent of the world's people do not have access to adequate sanitation necessary for daily life.[4] The trends are not changing for the better, and thus do not indicate hope for the future. While there are many positive developments in the world today, indications are that the next twenty to fifty years will continue with many of these numbers moving in the wrong direction. These trends have profound missiological implications. How should missionaries respond in light of these realities?

When looking to the future and considering the role of missions, it is helpful to pause and ask what churches, mission agencies and missionaries should be doing everywhere all the time. The answer we get depends on who we ask. For some, the work of proclamation and sharing the gospel is the only legitimate role for missions. Others believe that the priority of proclamation should be coupled with mercy ministries to meet human needs, such as drilling water wells, water purification, feeding the hungry, improving agricultural techniques, rescuing those trapped in flesh trafficking or providing health care. Still others would say that all of these ministries are legitimate Christian mission efforts— whether coupled with gospel proclamation or not.

When considering the mission of the church, some are confused by the difference between *mission* and *missions.* These words are sometimes used synonymously and there is little uniformity in missions literature, though technically the distinction between them is that *mission* (singular) refers to all the church is to do in the world, and *missions* (plural) refers to the diverse methods of

churches and missionaries to carry that out—evangelism, discipleship and church planting to extend the kingdom. The general
mission of the church is to worship God, glorify Christ, make disciples of all nations, baptize believers and teach them to obey all that
Christ has commanded. The many different ways that churches
engage the world for this ministry and purpose are too numerous to
mention, let alone describe in detail, but together they comprise missions. Do not get bogged down in the difference between terms like
missio Dei (mission of God), mission of the church and all the missions efforts of the church. The greater question for now is, What has
Christ commissioned his church to do in this world until he comes?

In recent decades various scholars have addressed and re-
addressed the biblical basis of mission and the relative value of the
many different expressions of missions in the world. Indeed, this
perennial concern continues to resurface as new waves of philosophies, strategies and methodologies splash onto the beach of missions. In the 1970s John Stott was so concerned about a potential
shift away from biblical missions that he delivered a series of lec-
tures which eventually became the book *Christian Mission in the
Modern World*.[5]

David Hesselgrave also wrote on ministry balance in missions.
His book *Paradigms in Conflict* was designed to introduce students
and missionaries to ten major paradigms that repeatedly create
controversy and division among missionaries. His goal was not to
drive one perspective but rather to explain both sides of each position and encourage missionaries to develop informed, biblically
defensible opinions. One issue Hesselgrave discusses is the mission
of the church. Instead of presenting a binary system that forces a
choice between either gospel proclamation or social ministry, Hesselgrave presents four points on a continuum. He first presents the
traditional view of pure gospel proclamation as a proper expression
of missions, calling it "prioritism theology." Next, he presents

restrained holism, which uses social ministry to open doors or provide a platform for the goal of gospel proclamation. Revisionist holism, on the other hand, views gospel proclamation and social ministry as equal partners; neither is more important than the other or truly distinguished from one another. Finally, he presents the radical perspective, "liberation theology," which is social ministry that may not even involve gospel proclamation because social justice and shalom on the earth are the essential aims of missions.[6]

Another key work that addresses the mission of the church is Kevin DeYoung and Greg Gilbert's *What Is the Mission of the Church?*[7] They argue through an exegetical treatment of pertinent biblical passages that much of what churches and even missionaries are doing today is good to do, but not technically the mission of the church, which they would define as primarily to make disciples. Some argue that including social ministry and community engagement is not only helpful but actually essential if the church is to faithfully represent Christ in the world today. A Haitian proverb teaches that a hungry stomach has no ears; thus even for the evangelist, some aspect of social ministry is effective and beneficial.

Reaching the Unreached Versus Making Disciples

The burden we feel for the lost is increased when we consider the growing awareness today of entire people groups who are unreached with the gospel, unengaged by any church planting effort and have never been contacted with the purpose of evangelization. Even after almost two thousand years of missions, over half of the world's people groups are considered unreached. These unreached people groups represent over one-third of the world's population. This is an astounding reality when we consider how quickly Coca-Cola went from its invention in 1896 to being recognized by 95 percent of the world's population today. Our weak efforts are even more startling when we consider how quickly the Internet has covered and changed virtually every aspect of our world in the few short decades of its existence. So many innovations have managed to advance globally for profit, yet Christian expansion has not grown at nearly the same rate. Even though we are fighting against our sin nature and the prince of this world, surely we must admit that our efforts hardly reflect the kind of commitment that should correspond to the significance of a person's soul and the glory of Christ.

Someone has said that if Christianity is one-tenth as true as we claim, we should be ten times more excited about it than we are. Twenty centuries after Christ, untold millions are still unreached. The grievous burden we feel when we think of the thousands of people groups sitting in darkness should drive us to pray for them and for those who are trying to reach them. Even so, it is a terrible mistake with eternal consequences to reduce missions to a formula such as "Missions equals reaching the unreached," especially if we do not clearly define what it means to reach them. Given the clear instructions in the Great Commission, we should not consider undiscipled people to be reached, as if discipling them is a subsequent step in Christian ministry. Those who have been discipled and taught to observe all that Christ commanded are truly reached. The tragedy of the world is not that it is unreached but that it is undiscipled.

So, what exactly does God call missionaries to do? Are we to reach all the unreached? Can we do this by preaching the good news in a one-week evangelistic crusade? Or are we to teach those we reach through preaching? In the Great Commission Jesus called us to go and make disciples of all people groups (*panta ta ethnē*), to baptize them and to teach them to obey all he has commanded us. The question of the Great Commission should never be reduced to a dichotomy of reaching *or* teaching, but as two sides of the same coin. Our role is to reach *and* teach. It is clear from history that God calls and gifts some to dedicate themselves more to pioneer reaching and evangelism, while he gifts and calls others to teach and disciple. Perhaps this distinction results in some being called and Spirit guided to serve in certain areas where their gift is best utilized. However, never assume that reachers do not have to teach or teachers do not have to reach. Some indeed have the gift of evangelism, but we are all to evangelize. Some have the gift of giving, but we all are to give. In light of the needs of the world reality today and the coming realities racing toward us, how should we respond?

The struggle to balance reaching the unreached and discipling and teaching them should always be just that—a struggle. When we capitulate to a predetermined decision independent of the specific and particular facts of a given context, we have lost balance. Every missionary looking to the future and considering the needs of the hour feels the tension of knowing his or her role in the face of the surrounding realities. Certainly, God both leads his people and sovereignly determines every event they encounter (Ephesians 1:11). He also guides by an awareness of needs, personal gifts and opportunities, and by giving his people the desires of their hearts when they are delighting themselves in him.

The need for speed that drives some missions efforts today causes them to streamline the missionary task to something humanly manageable, and sometimes jettisons the half of the Great Commission that requires missionaries to stay and teach the people all God has commanded them. On the other hand, a desire to always be "the teacher" and not entrust nationals with the work keeps some missionaries from moving on to reach others. There is no formula, biblical or otherwise, that would give clear direction regarding the whos and wheres and whens. The Holy Spirit guides Christians to the places and ministries God has prepared in advance for each one of us (Ephesians 2:10), and he alone should be the one to move them on.

BIBLICAL PERSPECTIVE

The mission of God is found within his Word. The Bible is the unchanging Word of God. While there are many applications of the Word in thousands of specific situations among the many people groups of the world, there is only one meaning. In a world where everything is changing and change seems to be the only constant, God never changes. Whatever he has said to his people in the past is still applicable to us today—in every culture and in every era of history. How to apply his Word in faithful ways that are also culturally sensitive is the realm of cultural anthropology and applied missiology. However, the redemptive purposes of God do not change; every person must repent of their sin, submit to Christ as Lord and be born again. As future changes bring anxiety and scrambling to keep up in the offices of many missions agencies and the plans of countless missionaries, we can all rest on the unchanging fact that everyone needs to hear the gospel and be born again. God wants all people to worship him. As John Piper has said, "Missions exists because worship doesn't."[8]

The mission of God is first discovered in knowing God. What would we know about God if he had never revealed himself in the Bible? David tells us in Psalm 19:1-4 that we would know there is a Creator, but we would know little else. Paul picks up on this idea in Romans 1:18-20 and tell us that because God has revealed himself in the general revelation of nature, all are without excuse for not worshiping him as he demands. Paul continues in Romans 2:14-15 and tells us that we would also know that we have sinned against God. God has given us a conscience that condemns us, a heart with his law written upon it that testifies against our willful rebellion, and a rational mind that can discern whether something is good or bad. Every one of us knows that there is a Creator and that we have sinned against him. We also know that we will live for eternity somewhere (Ecclesiastes 3:11), and this is reflected in every culture.

There is simply no such thing as an honest atheist or a person who truly believes that he or she has never sinned. This is the heart of why we fear death. This is not going to change in the future, no matter how many sweeping changes blow through our world. The world's people need to hear the gospel message, repent and be born again. That is the only hope for our crippling guilt, and this good news brings the forgiveness and eternal life we desperately need.

The mission of God finds root and deepening expression as those who follow him walk with him, remaining sensitive and obedient to his leadership. When a person is born again, that is just the beginning of his or her Christian experience. Believers must begin the process of progressive sanctification whereby they learn to walk in the Spirit, saying no to the wrong and yes to the right. This process is complete in God's eyes at the moment of salvation due to the vicarious suffering of our substitute and the transfer of his holiness to our account in a great exchange. Yet we learn to pursue actual righteousness and a life of holiness as we walk with him. This process is not automatic in a fallen world. The Bible teaches us what pleases God and also what grieves his heart. We understand and follow the mission of God as we begin to know him more deeply. What we can know about God is most fully revealed in his Word. For this reason, studying God's Word is essential to be faithful to his mission.

The Bible is filled with commands instructing those who know God's Word to teach those who come behind by discipling, mentoring and modeling what God requires. When believers begin to grow in grace and thankfulness for the salvation they have freely received, they long to see others find the peace and hope they have. A desire to share the gospel with others, reaching and teaching those who are lost and undiscipled, is a natural development in the life of a growing disciple. This is amplified by the crises of natural and manmade disasters and the darkness of false religions in the world. A heart that breaks with the things that break the heart of God is shattered by lostness and religious confusion. Such broken hearts long for those trapped in hopelessness to hear the gospel and to learn to know, love and obey Christ. They long to disciple those who can teach others in culturally appropriate and biblically faithful ways. This is the mission of God.

Anticipating the Future

In the future, missions will have to adjust to countless new trends, technologies, crises and epidemics. New strategies and methods will have to be devised to meet the challenges faced. However, no matter what comes down the road or what adjustments have to be made for the church and missionaries to be relevant and effective, we must continue to reach the unreached and then teach them to obey all that Christ has commanded. Disciple-making strategies and methods must always be adjusted to the cultural realities of diverse cultures.

How will missionaries plant churches in countries where evangelical organizations are not legal or are not permitted to own property? Missionaries have rediscovered that churches may meet in houses or office buildings, remembering that some of the first churches met in prisons and catacombs. Shrinking missions budgets require more creativity. The house-church planting model has grown in popularity in many places around the world. Yet only after such methods were utilized in some contemporary cultural contexts did missionaries learn that some people suspect religious groups that meet in homes to be cults. With the mass movements of people to the cities in our increasingly urbanized world, how will urban missionaries meet the need for planting sufficient numbers of churches where buildings are prohibited by law, cost prohibitive or even dangerous? These are just a few examples of trends facing missionaries today; these demand new and more effective church planting models that are both culturally appropriate and biblically faithful.

KEY PRINCIPLES AND APPLICATION

As we have noted, some things never change. God never changes, his Word never changes and the meaning of his Word never changes. Another constant is the tug on our hearts as we think about the needs of the world. But the ways we deliver his Word, the buildings we meet in, the languages we speak, the music we use for worship and the literacy levels among the people vary from context to context. We find ourselves in the throes of finding out what it all means.

It has been said that when a child says thank you for the first time without prompting, he or she is well on the way to social maturity. In like fashion, when a new believer first asks God whether he wants him or her to serve as a missionary, this believer is well on the way to spiritual maturity. It demonstrates selflessness and a desire for many to fall at Jesus' feet and worship him as Lord.

The corporate effort to reach and teach the world for Christ's sake constitutes the majority of missions work around the world. Missionaries have had to adjust to new world realities that changed the way they have done missions. Moravian missionaries wanted to reach the African slaves working the sugar plantations of the Caribbean, but were forced to find other access to the slaves when the owners would not permit mission work among the slaves. Countries regularly close their doors to traditional missionaries, forcing missionaries to find creative-access platforms to obtain visas in order to minister in the countries where God has called them. As we step into the future, we must find creative ways to minister in new global realities that often challenge and impede traditional missions efforts. And we must remain faithful to God's Word in every respect as we do so.

The Holy Spirit is calling people from around the world to join in missions throughout the world, such as the Back to Jerusalem movement in China or the Latinos who are called to the Muslim world. Therefore, missionary training programs must be developed that will help these believers to fulfill their missionary call effectively.[9] Sometimes couples nearing retirement or who are empty nesters want to finish well and serve in missions. Perhaps a businessman has made his mark and all the money he needs to make to be successful and wonders how he could be involved in missions other than "pay, pray and get out of the way." Mission agencies must prepare to meet the future as it comes by providing opportunities for these men and women to be engaged in missions in areas of creative access and effective sending models.

CONCLUSION

Jesus told his church that we are to go and make disciples of all people groups, baptize them and teach them everything he has commanded. Each of the four Gospels and the book of Acts has some version of the Great Commission. The last command of Christ should be the first priority of his followers. To make disciples, we must engage the world as it is and preach the gospel. Engaging the world as it is means adjusting as it changes, not allowing our methods to become fossilized. When we are fossilized in ways of the past, trying to reach and teach people as we imagine them to be, wish them to be or as they once were, we miss the opportunities God gives.

Business and financial analysts, along with government foreign-policy experts, constantly watch the world with their finger on its pulse to monitor developments and trends—actual and potential. Some businesses and governments hire consultants to advise adjustments so they can meet challenges and continue past success. Becoming so enamored with the way we used to do it, or wishing the world were still as it once was in some golden era, inevitably results in being left behind. While it is important for global businesses and governments to be advised and aware of coming changes and challenges, it is eternally and infinitely more important for missionaries and the church of Jesus Christ to be prepared for the future, meet it head-on and engage it with effective strategies and methods. Only by anticipating the future, studying trends and considering the missiological implications will we be able to maximize missions efforts for success while advancing the kingdom and bringing glory to Christ. Now let's find out what these trends are and how we can meet the future with confidence.

Urbanization and Globalization

THE WORLD'S PEOPLES HAVE LIVED in cities since Cain built the first one and named it after his son (Genesis 4). And the dynamics of globalization have been growing since the first nation lived near, traded with and battled another. Neither urbanization nor globalization is a recent occurrence, but the trending exponential growth of these two realities and the challenges they present to those ministering in their midst certainly are.

"Come preach for our New York Quichuas" was the invitation from an Ecuadorian friend who was now pastoring a Hispanic church in Queens, New York. I was lecturing in Manhattan Friday and Saturday and was glad to extend my stay to accept the invitation. Even though I had worked with this people group for years in Ambato and Quito, Ecuador, and had written dissertations and books about them, I was quite unprepared for the encounter. Many of the Quichuas in attendance were speaking Quichua and wearing traditional outfits from their home culture, but they were different inside. Their worldview had changed; they were familiar with a bigger world than their cousins living in isolated mountain communities in South America. They spoke some English, understood international travel and living, had children who were US citizens, depended more on hard currency in their daily lives, and had embraced US culture more than the others back home. They were still Quichuas and proud of it; indeed they were choosing to worship at a Quichua church—perhaps as a last vestige of and connection to who they really were—but they were very different from their relatives on the wind-swept mountain ranges in the rugged Andes. Certainly my Spanish and limited Quichua, my knowledge of their historical background, the geography of their places of origin, and the religious syncretism that has characterized Quichuas since the Spanish conquest would be helpful in ministering to them. However, I quickly saw that I was interacting with a different people group from the one I expected to find. The world seems to be racing to the cities.

The United Nations announced in 2011 that for the first time in history the world is now more urban than rural, and this trend shows no sign of easing.

> More than one half of the world population lives now in urban areas, and virtually all countries of the world are becoming increasingly urbanized. This is a global phenomenon that has nonetheless very different expressions across regions and development levels: richer countries and those of Latin America and the Caribbean have already a large proportion of their population residing in urban areas, whereas Africa and Asia, still mostly rural, will urbanize faster than other regions over the coming decades. These trends are changing the landscape of human settlement, with significant implications for living conditions, the environment and development in different parts of the world.[1]

Urbanization presents significant challenges to missionaries, who historically have been more successful in rural areas and have seen much less fruit in cities. Missionaries are now asking themselves what changes need to be made to reach the lost, plant churches and make disciples in the cities, realizing that all this must be accomplished among new urban tribes, unprecedented demographics, gated communities and mobile populations.

Likewise, globalization presents unique challenges to missionaries. As cultural worlds collide in increasing measure due to international travel, trade and interconnectivity, people groups continually morph and shift. Cultural realities that have defined and described each region's traditional populations, including their religions, languages, music styles, education systems, forms of government, and their ethnicity's peculiar customs and orientations, are changing; they influence and are influenced by every group they interact with. This phenomenon of shifting and evolving cultural mosaics results in a moving target for missionaries. They struggle and strategize to find keys to unlock the doors of effective ministry in an area, but find themselves looking for new keys before ever finding the first set because the doors and locks are constantly changing. Imagine trying to develop a friendship with someone whose personality changes daily. This chapter will address some key issues of the challenges of urbanization and globalization, and suggest perspectives to keep in mind for these contexts.

TRENDING URBAN

The growth of world cities has continued unabated since the beginning of the Industrial Revolution (1760–1840). The United Nations reports, "More than half of the world population lives in urban areas. Nevertheless, not all regions of the world have reached this level of urbanization." According to the UN's *World Urbanization Prospects*, "it is expected that half of the population of Asia will live in urban areas by 2020, while Africa is likely to reach a 50 per cent urbanization rate only in 2035."[2]

The trend for the future of cities around the world has yielded new terminology. Statisticians and demographers now routinely speak of *megacities*, cities with more than ten million inhabitants. *National Geographic* reported in 2014, "Sixty years ago in 1950, there were only two megacities—New York-Newark and Tokyo. In 1995, 14 megacities existed. Today, there are 22, mostly in the developing countries of Asia, Africa and Latin America. By 2025, there will probably be 30 or more."[3] *Forbes* reported that trending urbanization is predominant in non-Western nations, where birth rates outpace those of developing nations. This will result in reduced influence and relevance of Western nations in the future. *Forbes* reported,

> This de-Westernizing trend seems likely to continue. The fastest-growing megacities over the past decade have been primarily in the developing world. Karachi, Pakistan, has led the growth charge, with a remarkable 80% expansion in its population from 2000 to 2010. The growth economies of China and India dominate the rest of the list of most rapidly growing megacities. . . . So what do the numbers tell us about the future of megacities? For one thing, it's clear that the most rapid growth is taking place in countries that still have large rural hinterlands and relatively young populations.[4]

The places where urbanization is growing most quickly seem to correlate closely with the growth of population in general. By 2050 the countries with the greatest number of inhabitants will be India, China, Nigeria, United States, Indonesia, Pakistan and Brazil.[5]

URBAN CHALLENGES

Burgeoning urban populations and the overcrowding of cities create challenges for governments as well as for missionaries. As a city's population grows, the need for transportation and daily commuting grows, resulting in traffic congestion. Additionally, increasing numbers of vehicles quickly saturate a city beyond the point that its streets were designed to handle, resulting in accidents, air pollution, and the mundane frustrations and economic strain of productivity lost to traffic delays and parking challenges. To combat this growing problem some cities have adopted new city ordinances that limit the days on which certain vehicles may be operated in the city. Citizens of means are increasingly hiring drivers, allowing them to work from the car during traffic-snarled commutes and eliminating the need to park and walk. Additionally, the concomitant rise in crime that accompanies population growth and overcrowding has resulted in some executives hiring drivers who are also trained bodyguards.

As cities grow in population, they often grow vertically. Highrise apartment buildings are the logical model for new construction in crowded cities where a few single-family homes would occupy the same footprint. With high-rise apartment dwellings come armed guards at street entrances and overprotective maids who can virtually isolate a family from any unsolicited interaction, effectively limiting access to the families who live there. Even in traditional neighborhoods with single-family homes and manicured lawns, the phenomenon of gated-communities that require permission to enter is universal. All of these realities are challenges to the missionaries who long to reach a city's residents. Missionaries must find effective and creative ways to engage city dwellers cocooned in their isolated microenvironments.

Realities in the cities are often scale model versions of the country in general. Within a city it is fairly easy to identify the economic inequalities and distinguish between the haves and havenots. The wealthy neighborhoods are clearly distinguished from the slums and other subtler levels of socioeconomic class distinctions, which may be discerned by noticing the quality of the houses, year and make of the vehicles, deterioration of buildings, evidence of gang presence, and other indicators. Initially, ethnic group immigrants may reside in specific areas of town, such as Little Italy and Chinatown, but eventually people begin to move beyond these confines. The realities of rising crime, socioeconomic challenges or political realities may bring more adhesion between ethnic group immigrants and their neighbors than the ethnic identity they share with people back home.

Some urban missiologists have labeled this phenomenon *urban tribes*, which are segments of society made up of peoples in a common area of a city, whether or not any ethnic or DNA connection exists between them. This idea is controversial, owing to the broad brush used to paint the portrait defining an urban tribe. Generally speaking, it is a group of people in a city who share a particular lifestyle or interest, and it is clear that different sections of cities have ties that bind. An urban neighborhood or city block may contain residents whose parents or grandparents came from Italy, Guatemala, Puerto Rico, Turkey, Pakistan, China and Bosnia, and who may find nothing in common with each other at first. In the beginning of their relationship, they may prefer to socialize and interact with relatives or others from their home country. However after years in the neighborhood with all their children in the same public school, hearing the political rhetoric during local elections, recognizing the danger from growing crime, seeing gang graffiti on the school building and storefronts, and hearing neighbors complaining about the potholes in the streets, the community begins to bond around a common cause. It is not surprising to find that daily life often trumps ancestry for what really matters. Residents often resonate more with their new city neighbors than they do with their rural cousins in the home country. To this degree the idea of urban tribe is alive and well, and the missionary's task is complicated.

URBAN MISSIONS

No matter the degree to which the residents in an area of town feel connected to one another in an urban tribe, they present the missionary with the challenge of a highly mobile and crowded population. Each culture has a background and worldview for interaction with others that remains intact until they begin to assimilate and acculturate. In addition to the linguistic and cultural challenges, missionaries must take into account peoples' diverse levels of allegiance to traditional religious backgrounds and worldviews.

Missionaries serving in communities or villages throughout the scattered corners of the world often spend their lives learning languages and making friends with the gatekeepers of a single culture. However, when visiting an urban context in a Western city and meeting people from that same people group, the missionaries realize that these urban people are different from those the missionaries minister among in their native country. These people have changed as they have adjusted to life in a new city and country. There is great benefit in knowing their heart language and original worldview, but this urban reality presents new challenges. The immigrants have adopted some aspects of the new culture and some aspects of their neighbors' preferences, and are beginning to think and process information using a new language. Yes, knowing their background and where they came from is helpful, but the missionaries recognize that they cannot import wholesale the ministry strategy and methods used in another country and apply them to the urbanized immigrants who live in community with people from a variety of countries.

Cultures living in close proximity and interacting on a regular basis are like the ingredients of a stew, each takes some of the flavor of the other ingredients and yields some of its own in the process. The overall flavor is unique, consisting of all the ingredients, which are still recognizable, but everything has changed somewhat. This intercultural stew creates yet another manifestation of the urban tribe mentioned earlier. Urban missionaries or church planters should not use methods and strategies to reach new immigrants as if they were typical US citizens. They will benefit by having some familiarity with all the cultures present, the urban tribe dynamics and the ever-changing aspects of the mixture.

Leaders in the business and political worlds develop people profiles in this developing urban growth. Marketing campaigns focus on demographic realities, average incomes, and the products and prices each group would find attractive. Relevant products are targeted to specific areas. Politicians focus their speeches on the needs of particular areas and tailor each speech to the specific context. Missionaries would do well to learn from these examples. The content of the missionaries' message never changes; the way it is delivered should always do so. Speaking German to Mandarin speakers is pointless. Paul's lesson in 1 Corinthians 9:20-23, of becoming "all things to all people" for the sake of winning them, should be applied to our ministry in each urban context we enter.

Ethnic dividing lines do not necessarily define the haves and have-nots in the cities. Even Hollywood has for decades anticipated the future of our planet, depicting it with peoples of all races and ethnic backgrounds living in huge urban areas where the privileged few have life pretty easy while others live a hellish existence in abject poverty, scratching out an existence surrounded by crime. Movies such as *Soylent Green* and *Elysium* show a wealthy class and a struggling worker class in such stark distinction that one may doubt whether the human race could ever sink so low, but many trapped in today's inner cities undoubtedly feel that such a reality is quickly on the way, if not already here.

Another challenge urbanization presents missionaries and church planters is how to reach the influential peoples in any society. These are the families and individuals among the new rich, old rich, politicians, high-ranking military officers, soccer stars and even powerful criminal elements. People at this level of society find that they must isolate their lives to protect their privacy, their families, their money and their safety. Reaching them effectively requires missionaries to live a similar socioeconomic lifestyle in order to fit in their circles. Peoples in this segment of society often feel empowered by their wealth, connections and positions. This sense of power and control may create a defiant, independent spirit that is closed to any spiritual need, believing that they can handle anything that comes their way. In order to be there to speak into their lives when things fall apart, causing them to realize that they were living a delusion, missionaries must live in proximity to them, develop relationships with them and earn their trust even in the midst of a perceived lack of need. Such proximity in lifestyle and residence requires much larger budgets and often living above the missionaries' accustomed reality. Similarly, I have often explained to missionaries who will be working among the poor that they must discipline themselves to live like those they are trying to reach as much as is possible. Even the most basic lifestyle of a typical US citizen in a Third World, urban poor environment can appear lavish to those we are seeking to reach, just as the lifestyles of the influentials appear to the typical Western missionary.

TRENDING GLOBAL

The growth of megacities is not only due to the movement from the rural areas of countries to the capital cities, it is also fueled by the globalization of our world. As previously noted, the world's peoples are highly mobile. Increased interconnectivity facilitates an openness to and often the need to travel. Missiologists' growing interest in diaspora missions is due to the fact that increasing numbers of people now live outside the country of their birth, where they find work, education and eventually a home. Globalization is not a new

concept, but it is growing in its speed and impact. The World Health
Organization defines the phenomenon as

> the increased interconnectedness and interdependence of
> peoples and countries, [and] is generally understood to
> include two interrelated elements: the opening of borders
> to increasingly fast flows of goods, services, finance,
> people and ideas across international borders; and the
> changes in institutional and policy regimes at the interna-
> tional and national levels that facilitate or promote such
> flows. It is recognized that globalization has both positive
> and negative impacts on development.[6]

The influence and interaction of peoples sharing the same
space changes the way traditional missionaries must carry out their
work. Immigration changes the cultural mosaic of the places where
they live. In the United States immigration is affecting countless
communities. The Migration Policy Institute reports,

> Nearly 41 million immigrants lived in the United States in
> 2012—a historical numeric high for a country that has
> been a major destination for international migrants
> throughout its history. About 20 percent of all interna-
> tional migrants reside in the United States, which ac-
> counts for less than 5 percent of the world's population.[7]

In 2013 I was in London to research the levels of assimilation
of peoples who have immigrated there from the Americas and the
Caribbean. The findings in that demographic were not as dramatic
as the startling numbers of Muslims and Hindus who have immigrated to London. Indeed, in 2013 the name Muhammad became
London's most popular baby name for boys.[8] Clearly, a missionary
living and working in London without taking into account the rise
in Muslim immigrants would be missing the mark. Another lesson

learned from that ethnographic research is that although global-ization is giving rise to a world village in many ways, the world is not adopting a common culture. The obvious differences among the preferences in dress, food, music and religions of London's peoples are clear evidence that the world's cultural diversity is not threatened by globalization.

The vitality of the world's thousands of languages may not be as noticeable among world travelers and immigrants who publically use English, French, Spanish or whatever the local lingua franca happens to be. Yet the world's languages will continue in strength to the degree that they are spoken in the home. Many US public school systems must interact with student's parents who speak other lan-guages. Indeed, in Louisville, Kentucky, the school system has a student body that uses over one hundred languages in their homes. If anything, the globalization of the world is increasing interest in other languages as well as facilitating easier access to learn them.

International students are also living and studying in the United States, United Kingdom and all around the world in an effort to get the best education they can. Over one and a half million interna-tionals are in the United States alone on student visas or as depen-dents.[9] While most may return home upon graduation, many do not. The fact that they remain in the United States not only affects the communities where they settle; sadly there is often a tragic impact on the countries they left. Since the brightest and best are often the ones who qualify for admission to universities, can obtain the nec-essary visas and have the connections to make it all happen, their failure to return home after graduation is keenly felt. This brain drain is an unfortunate reality throughout the developing nations.

GLOBALIZATION CHALLENGES

The challenges for missionaries in the face of globalization are as myriad as the benefits. On the positive side there is greater mobility and global interconnectivity, which makes the world seem a more manageable place. Missionaries no longer need to be concerned with leaving home for the mission field and being cut off from family, friends and Christian fellowship for years at a time. Internet communication and international travel have resulted in a highly mobile world that is in constant communication. Call the 800 number on the back of your credit card and very likely a pleasant voice at a call center in India will answer the phone. When you travel internationally, try to guess the national origins of the other passengers in the gate area preparing to board the plane. It is increasingly harder to do with all the international businesses, vacation spots and educational opportunities that are scattering people around the world.

The downside of globalization is seen in the challenges it presents. For missionaries seeking visas to serve in creative-access countries on a visa platform other than Christian missions, the Internet greatly facilitates government access to social media history and other pertinent background details. It is virtually impossible to have a blank page come up when someone Googles your name. Even if this were possible, others connected to the missionary back home or in ministry settings on the field may be investigated using Internet searches and bring guilt by association. I was in a communist country and shared with my contact there about a ministry partner that I hoped to bring there on a future trip. I told some of his testimony and how he had been a US airman and was wounded in action. The story is pretty dramatic and it even garnered some press when it happened. My ministry contact in the country was genuinely interested but quickly warned me against bringing that person to his country. He said that since this had been in the press, it would be easy for government officials to see, and since the country the United States was fighting was an ally of his country, my ministry partner would be persona non grata when seeking to obtain a visitor's visa. I realized that many of the blessings that missionaries have from the globalization of our world have a negative side as well. Missionaries should consider the ease with which their backgrounds may be investigated, friends and family members identified, and how vulnerable they become when anyone hostile to their cause has their personal information. Anonymity is a thing of the past, and one's ministry experience can easily be found on the Web and seen by anyone.

Another challenge of the dynamic of globalization is the myth of the melting pot. When I was young, our teachers used to teach us that the United States is a melting pot: that all the peoples of the world's cultures come to the United States and meld into one vast new people called Americans. That, of course, is not true. We may be increasingly connected and well-traveled, even becoming one world village in many ways, but we are not one big culture. People groups may be living in close proximity, but they are retaining culturally distinctive aspects of who they are, such as language, dress, religion and family systems. The problem is that each person assimilates to greater or lesser degrees depending on factors such as local prejudice, whether they have come by refugee or immigrant status and employment opportunities.

When missionaries arrive on the field in their target countries, they are highly motivated to acculturate, learn the language, adapt to the rhythm of life, appreciate the cuisine and music, make friends, and identify with the local culture. Yet, even so, missionaries often find themselves staying home ordering pizza, eating at the American club with expatriate friends, and spending free time on Facebook, Twitter, blogs and websites from their home country just to recharge their batteries from the culture shock. Imagine the challenge for those who are not as highly motivated due to being displaced peoples, political refugees or even immigrants who have not had the opportunity to attend a language school or receive crosscultural orientation. The globalized mobile and interconnected world is not necessarily conducive to the development of positive experiences.

Missions in the Midst of Globalization

Since people tend to assimilate to greater or lesser degrees, peoples from the same people groups may be at vastly different positions on the assimilation or acculturation continuum. How should we define people groups in this age of globalization?

When Ralph Winter introduced the challenge of reaching "unreached people groups" at the Lausanne Conference for World Evangelization in 1974, the idea was somewhat new and therefore a little controversial. After all, most missionaries in the era of modern missions considered the Great Commission to be their marching orders, and Jesus says to make disciples of all nations. Since the common understanding of nations was geopolitical entities, the fact that there was a church or group of believers in every country on the globe seemed to indicate that the Great Commission had been accomplished. Winter pointed out the fallacy in this thinking and reminded them that in the New Testament's original Greek, Jesus had commissioned the church to make disciples in every people group. Yet even then the initial definition of people group was pretty basic: "For evangelistic purposes . . . [it] is 'the largest group within which the gospel can spread as a church planting movement without encountering barriers of understanding or acceptance.'"[10] The International Mission Board defines *people group* as "an *ethnolinguistic group* with a common self-identity that is shared by the various members. There are two parts to that word: *ethno*, and *linguistic*. Language is a primary and dominant identifying factor of a people group."[11] The Joshua Project adds a helpful qualifier,

> In many parts of the world lack of understandability serves as the main barrier and it is appropriate to define

people groups primarily by language with the possibility of sub-divisions based on dialect or cultural variations. In other parts of the world, most notably in portions of South Asia, acceptance is a greater barrier than understandability. In these regions, caste, religious tradition, location, common histories and legends, plus language may be used to define the boundaries of each people group. Joshua Project uses the terms "people," "people group" and "ethnic people" synonymously. However, others may distinguish between the terms.[12]

All of the distinctions and improvements to the definitions that have been contributed through the years add greater understanding but fail to settle all the discussions related to defining people groups.

Globalization has added more confusion to the discussion of people groups since peoples from similar places of origin, ancestry, language, religion, worldview, culture and affinity change as they assimilate to greater or lesser degrees. In their home country a people group may have a healthy church, their own New Testament, some discipled members, trained leaders and a biblically faithful, critically contextualized church that is culturally appropriate. Yet those who immigrated over several decades had to leave their homes because they were displaced, persecuted or faced economic pressures. In some cases those who moved did not continue to practice Christianity for a variety of possible reasons: lack of a preacher/teacher, no literate persons among them to guide them in the Word, no desire for religion or simply the 24/7 struggle to stay alive in a new country. An urban missionary conducting research in the United States may find that there are no Christians among this people group in his or her urban context. Further research reveals that there is no church among this people group anywhere in the United States. Are they an unreached people group? Some missiologists say yes and others say no. Globalization challenges missionaries to reckon with new expressions or far-flung segments of existing people groups. There may not be clear-cut answers to these questions, but the possibility of interacting with missionaries who obtained cultural knowledge from working with them in other countries would certainly be helpful, although we must realize that what was effective in one context may not work in another.

CLASSIFYING MINISTRY

Missionaries need to be cognizant of the need to research each ministry context and not categorize or stereotype peoples because of appearance, language or ethnic descriptor. When ministers in Anglo churches in the United States tell me that they are starting a Hispanic outreach or mission, I always ask to which Hispanics. This usually elicits a confused reaction and the response, "To those who speak Spanish." When I ask which Spanish speakers specifically, they often realize that I am getting to a point and begin to listen. I point out that twenty-two countries speak Spanish, and each one of them has numerous people groups. Some have well over a hundred people groups, with reached and unreached, literate and oral learners, and wealthy and impoverished peoples. To which group are they reaching out? Obviously the globalization of the world is mobilizing people from around the world and from all walks of life to go throughout the world. A church in Italy reaching out to the US citizens who have moved to their country should keep in mind that those from Cajun Louisiana are different from those hailing from Massachusetts, and those from Los Angeles are different from those from the Bronx. Although all may be US citizens and speak English, they often have different preferences in music, food, leadership styles and priorities. Anglo churches in the United States beginning a Hispanic mission in a part of town with both Cubans and Mexicans will likely find within a very few months that they have either a Mexican church or a Cuban church due to the striking differences between those groups.

Globalization challenges the traditional terms used to determine race or ethnicity and renders them increasingly unhelpful. Consider the terms *race, ethnicity* and *culture*, and you will see that each is hard to define, and one person's definition may not be clearly understood by another. Likewise, the uninformed assumption that all Hispanics are Mexicans, come from hot, arid areas and eat Tex-Mex is extremely offensive. This unfortunate caricature has spawned the popularity of a T-shirt design bearing the flag of different Latin American countries and the slogan, "I'm Not Mexican!" Just as Mexicans are proud to be from Mexico, those from other countries identify with their home countries.

The Census Bureau states, "'Hispanic or Latino' refers to a person of Cuban, Mexican, Puerto Rican, South or Central American, or other Spanish culture or origin regardless of race."[13] The term *Hispanic* was actually invented by the US government for use in the census, and has not been without confusion or controversy ever since. "The term Hispanic as used in the USA, was coined by the U.S. Census Bureau in the 1970s to describe people of Spanish-speaking origin. It is not a term that originated from within the culture. Primarily people who have been formed and educated in the USA use Hispanic. They are accustomed to the term by education or by family custom. Latin American nationals, recent immigrants to this country, will not self-identify as *Hispanic*."[14]

The U.S. Census Bureau has the daunting task of identifying the national background and ethnicity of everyone living in the United States every ten years. It is not only difficult to identify and employ terms that clearly communicate to all, the meanings of the terms themselves keep changing along with descriptor preference of those described.[15] *Hispanic* is not the only problematic term, according to Census officials Nicholas Jones and Roberto Ramirez. "'Increasingly, Americans are saying they cannot find themselves' on census forms, Jones said. Many communities, including Hispanics, Arabs and people of mixed race, have said they're unsure of how to identify themselves on census forms."[16]

"American Indians," "First Nations People," "Native Americans" and "Red Indians" have all been used to describe the peoples who lived in North America prior to the arrival of Europeans, and each term has been found to be offensive at one time or another through the years. Of course, it would be better to define them as Blackfoot, Choctaw, Cherokee or Hopi and so forth, but with hundreds of nations it is difficult to know exactly which one to use or how to describe those who have intermarried with other indigenous groups or other ethnicities. My great-great-grandmother was Choctaw— and both my great-grandmother and my grandmother looked it. My mother favored her Irish father more than the Choctaw coloring of my grandmother, and I took after my mother and father. I have always been proud of my American Indian heritage and am quick to point it out, but it would not be accurate to consider myself American Indian, nor would anyone mistake me to be. Globalization is bringing similar shifts and blurring of lines within many groups around the world, and it does not only happen with DNA and language.

Some religions of the world have preserved their purity through the ages with enforced endogamy. An endogamous group is one in which its members must marry from within the group. Historically, Jewish people were so because God's Word taught them not to intermarry with the nations. Solomon was warned not to take foreign wives because they would lead him to worship their gods. Unfortunately, Solomon did, and they did as God had warned. In Nehemiah's day, during his rebuilding of Jerusalem's walls after the Babylonian exile, he found that some of the Jewish people had intermarried with women from the surrounding nations, and retribution was swift and unyielding.

> In those days also I saw the Jews who had married women of Ashdod, Ammon, and Moab. And half of their children spoke the language of Ashdod, and they could not speak the language of Judah, but only the language of each people. And I confronted them and cursed them and beat some of them and pulled out their hair. And I made them take an oath in the name of God, saying, "You shall not give your daughters to their sons, or take their daughters for your sons or for yourselves. Did not Solomon king of Israel sin on account of such women? Among the many nations there was no king like him, and he was beloved by his God, and God made him king over all Israel. Nevertheless, foreign women made even him to sin. Shall we then listen to you and do all this great evil and act treacherously against our God by marrying foreign women?" (Nehemiah 13:23-27)

The intermarrying of peoples from different religious background not only affects the religious commitment and practice of those who marry, it influences the likelihood of whether their children will follow their particular religion.

Not only does intermarriage impact religious identification and expression, so does merely living in close proximity to people groups. While geography and distance from the homeland seem easily overcome by those fervently committed to a given religion, some regions of the world seem to carry a secularizing force. Europe has long been noted as such an area of the world. As peoples have moved to countries in Western Europe, their religious practices are often mitigated or blunted after time in its pluralistic context.

In the Americas, the Spanish Conquest brought Catholicism to the countries of what is now Latin America, where most people

strongly identify as Catholics, but it is very common to find a syncretism of Catholicism and indigenous animism. Some missiologists
refer to this ubiquitous syncretism as Christopaganism or Christi-
animism. While there was no desire on the part of the faithful to
change the beliefs of Roman Catholicism, centuries of living among
animists, intermarrying, practicing both religions in families and
finding expressions of both in virtually every part of the society, the
resulting unholy mixture is fact. After a consideration of Catholicism in both Latin America and other regions, Pope John Paul II
called for a new evangelization.[17] Kevin Cotter reported on the need:

> So, what is the new evangelization? Blessed John Paul II
> describes a situation between the first two options "where
> entire groups of the baptized have lost a living sense of the
> faith, or even no longer consider themselves members of
> the Church, and live a life far removed from Christ and his
> Gospel. In this case what is needed is a 'new evangeli-
> zation' or a 're-evangelization.'"[18]

This is very clear in areas where Catholicism is so mixed with offerings
to indigenous deities, veneration of spirits and practices of shamanism
that orthodox Roman Catholicism would scarcely recognize it.

Among Vietnamese immigrants where I have supervised ethnographic research, Buddhists and Catholics are often found at each
other's religious services and rituals. The cultural bond with others
who share the same food, language, music, historical heritage and
DNA is strong enough to allow them to set religious differences
aside at times. In many cultures and among many religions this has
resulted in a blurring of the lines and beliefs between groups.

CONCLUSION

Isolation is one way to safeguard the purity of race, language and
religion, yet that is increasingly difficult and ill-advised in the age

of urbanization and globalization. The crashing together of world-views and cultures results in a global stew that changes the ingredients as they steep. As worldviews come into contact with one another, they shift and adapt. Just as cultures interacted on the Silk Road, they interact today, only at blinding speeds and with staggering complexity. Missionaries must be aware of the innumerable manifestations of the cultures they serve, depending on where the inhabitants live, the peoples living nearby, the exposure to the Internet, the ages of the peoples involved and the desire of each group to assimilate or not. It is no longer as simple as reaching Germans, Hispanics, Africans or Chinese peoples, if indeed it ever really was.

When there is only one language to learn, one new cuisine to acquire a taste for, one group of gatekeepers to meet and develop relationships with, and one worldview to understand, even then it is a lifelong task. When a missionary finds scores of these in one urban setting, it can be overwhelming. Knowledge of cultural backgrounds is helpful, but each group must be approached and understood in its own context.

Travel, Communication and the Missionary Life

WILLIAM CAREY, THE FATHER of modern missions, set the example for countless aspects of missionary life for generations to come. After he sailed to India for lifelong missionary service at the end of the eighteenth century, many followed his pattern of leaving home, believing that they would never see their loved ones on earth again. They sailed on tall ships to unknown countries to serve their target people groups. The pattern continued until relatively recent times. Indeed, many missionary families still on the field recount their own experience of initially leaving their home countries sailing on vessels that required weeks of travel to arrive at the port in their new mission field country.

The stories of early missionaries tell of tearful goodbyes to family and friends at the dock as they boarded ships for foreign fields. Providentially, their confinement onboard the ship gave them time to process their grief over having left all they ever knew and loved. As their ship traveled toward their destination, stopping at ports along the way to take on or deliver freight, they had time to dry their tears, embrace the reality of their call and experience an awakening excitement for the missionary life they were soon to begin.

Perhaps they perused grammar books for the language they would soon be studying full time, or they studied their Bibles and received God's encouragement by reading passages recounting Paul's missionary life. Perhaps they met someone onboard who was familiar with the country they sailed to serve and greedily quizzed them for every tidbit of information. Slowly but surely they passed through the adjustment from being grieving believers to becoming excited missionaries with a mature understanding and eagerness to begin missionary life. That was then.

Today's missionaries wave goodbye to Mom and Dad at the airport's security checkpoint, mouthing the words to Mom that they love her and will text her when they land. They board the flight for their country of service and land within hours rather than weeks. True to their word, they text their parents to let them know that they arrived safely and promise that they will call them later. The missionary who picks them up at the airport takes them to Burger King on the way to the mission guest apartment and tells them, over the familiarity of his favorite burger joint, that the guest house has an Internet-based telephone service so they can call their folks to let them know they arrived safely. Arriving at the guest apartment before bedtime they marvel that they were just waking up and eating breakfast with their folks in their home country that same day. To test the phone service, one picks up the receiver and calls his parents as if calling locally and tells them about their day. He promises to Skype the next day so that they can see one another. Before they turn in for the night they decide to check their email, Facebook and Twitter. They are pleasantly surprised to find several friends online and chat with them. Several unintended hours later they get to bed feeling as if they haven't even left the States.

SHIFTS OF TRAVEL

Missionaries have come a long way from the days of traveling on sailing ships, daring the dangers of pirate attacks and scurvy—or have we? Missionary travel is still rife with risk, as the many options available for international health and missionary life insurance testify. Indeed, missions travel is at least as dangerous today if not more so because it happens at the speed of jet travel and covers greater distances in shorter time spans. Although air travel is statistically one of the safest modes of transportation, every security checkpoint reminds us of the increased threat of terrorism, keeping us aware of travel's inherent dangers. The dangers from bad guys, whether pirates or terrorists, and the risk of disease, whether scurvy, malaria or some new strain of virus, bear witness to the fact that we still live in a fallen world and that there is nothing new under the sun.

The change in the speed and ease of travel is obvious and undeniable. Indeed, I am sometimes in several countries on several different continents in a single week's time. The relative cost of international travel makes the world seem a much smaller place than it did a couple of centuries ago. Even as I write this, I am on a plane headed to a Central American country to strategize with some missionaries and preach—just for the weekend. Several weeks ago I traveled for a couple of days to Brazil from my current home in the United States. Traveling such distances for such a short period of time would have staggered the imaginations of previous generations.

While the *Star Trek* generation has grown accustomed to depictions of the transporter beam teleporting Captain Kirk and First Officer Spock to distant locations in a few seconds' time, we know that it is science fiction. However, most of the show's fans have probably fantasized about how nice it would be to travel great distances so quickly—especially during a long vacation trip by car with preschoolers! What if missionaries had access to such technology and could "commute" to the mission field each morning and return home at the end of the day! It sounds wonderful at first, but how would that missionary learn the language and culture, build relationships, understand the worldview or relate deeply with the people? We have not yet attained such transporter beam technology, but to the degree that missionaries remain in their home culture and only go among their people group for brief periods, returning to the womb of their comfort zone with a technological umbilical cord, they will hinder their ability for effective missions service.

For centuries some of the brightest lights in the missionary sky were those men and women who went out young and returned to their homelands only for a short visit with supporting churches, friends and family—if they ever returned at all. It is not uncommon for today's missionaries to return once every year or two for visits of a few weeks or months. Regular return visits home—even the mere ability to do so should the desire arise—have changed the way missionaries face the hardships of life on the field. When the difficulties of language learning, culture shock, crime, corruption, homesickness or sickness from some disease unknown at home strikes, missionaries can easily daydream of a few months in the future when a clean, modern airliner awaits to whisk them to their home country and into the arms of loved ones. In past generations, hardships were not so easily escaped.

Missionaries stayed through it all. They learned the language and loved the people, lived among them as one of them, thus enabling them to understand the worldviews and find bridges over the barriers to bearing gospel fruit in their adopted homelands. Some missionaries actually went so far as to view themselves as immigrants to the new country, taking its citizenship, educating their children in the country's school system, buying property and retiring there. The challenge today lies in the opposite direction. Indeed, some missionaries have not fully left their home country.

In *Ministering Cross-Culturally,* Sherwood Lingenfelter wrote of the 150 percent human. He argued that no one can be a 200 percent person like Jesus was; the best any missionary could aspire to become is 150 percent. What he meant is that Jesus was 100 percent God, and in his incarnation became 100 percent human also, making him the only 200 percent person. Since we cannot enter another culture as a baby and grow up, experiencing all that someone would in that country, the best we can attain is about 75 percent. Lingenfelter wrote that to succeed in the endeavor, we must be willing to lose about 25 percent of who we are, such as former prejudices and preferences, rendering us a 150 percent human at best.[1]

When missionaries refuse to lose any of who they are or do not fully embrace the new country, they cannot identify with the people they seek to serve. Understanding their culture and worldview is essential for communicating the gospel in culturally appropriate ways and to be truly effective. An old saying teaches, "To sail to new worlds one must be willing to lose sight of shore." Those who never leave their home country—even in mind, desires, hopes or preferences—will never settle in and will always be marking time until the next visit back "home." Sadly, the nationals often know that before the missionary does.

Air travel is relatively cheap in comparison with the costs of all the days lost and dangers encountered in years past. In one of the locations where I take teams to teach in an Amazon jungle, the most common method of transportation readily available is river travel in motorized dugout canoes or peque-peques. Fuel costs in those areas, coupled with the realities of supply and demand, make the cost of river transport prohibitive for many of our pastors. And yet something tells me it won't always be that way. The more developed our world becomes, and the more companies compete for travelers' loyalty, the more affordable and user-friendly travel will become, and the smaller our world will seem. For missionaries leaving more developed countries, parting is less difficult when we know we will be back in a few months and could come back tomorrow if absolutely necessary.

Ease of travel has resulted in some mission agencies instituting policies limiting travel home until after the first term of service, usually three to four years. Others discourage return visits until after graduation from language school, and still others place limits on travel for the first year. This pattern reflects the prevailing wisdom that new missionaries need time to adjust to the realities of the new culture before returning to the comfort of the old—even for a short visit. Indeed, missionaries speak of "flipping a switch in their head" when they learn of the policy forbidding return visits during an initial period of their deployment. Just knowing that it was not an option kept them from entertaining the idea on difficult days.

Policies limiting return travel home during their adjustment period are wise but should be discussed well in advance, preferably in the early stage of the application process. Waiting to reveal such a policy until orientation could result in great disappointment or worse, especially for those who promised parents that they could come home to visit. Learning that this is not allowed for an initial period is best learned upfront—both for the missionary and family left behind—so as to avoid any mistaken assumptions that would be hard to handle later on.

Ease of travel has also multiplied the number of short-term mission (STM) trips. While some may be interested in merely serving as "vacationaries," many others are armed with solid pre-trip orientation, proper on-field leadership and post-trip debriefings that result in excellent missions education as well as great good accomplished in the field. They also serve and encourage both missionaries and their national partners. Indeed, in many cases the STM participants are able to do things that the field missionaries dare not do since the visitors can have a higher profile while in the country than the career field missionaries can—for example, participating openly in activities such as Bible distribution or gospel witnessing.

COMMUNICATION SHIFTS

William Carey and his contemporaries would have used quill pens to write long letters and send them by any ship headed toward their home countries, and then they waited months for a response. If a point in their letter was not clear or for some reason the recipient incorrectly understood the original letter, it would likely have resulted in a misinformed response to the field missionary. Years could be lost in the effort. Even a mere couple of decades ago there was no Internet access for instant communication with families, friends, churches and home offices. A missionary in the early 1990s would have written a letter and posted it with prayers that it would arrive at its intended destination. One missionary in Ecuador finally received a letter that had been mailed to him several months prior from the USA. It turned out that the postal service interpreted the SA at the bottom of the address to mean South Africa rather than South America, and the letter had to travel around the world before reaching the correct destination. Even if all worked as it should have and the recipient decided to answer a letter immediately, the letter would take two weeks to arrive and the response would have required the same time. The missionary needing direction or information would wait a month to get the answer.

In 1994, I listened to the administrator of our Ecuador mission with rapt attention as he explained a new form of correspondence called electronic mail. He said the US Army was already using this technology. A person could write a letter on a computer, and instead of printing and mailing it, he or she could simply send it over the telephone lines through cyberspace and the intended recipient would get it almost immediately. This sounded like pure science fiction and very dangerous since it seemed to me that anyone could read your mail. He assured me that passwords would be required to access the information, but I was dubious and told him I doubted that our agency would ever use such risky technology for our correspondence. (You might want to make a mental note not to seek my advice about technology investments.)

On special occasions such as a birthday, Christmas or Mother's Day, when we wanted to call long distance to speak to family members back home, we would go to the telephone company, give the receptionist the number we wanted to reach and then take a seat in the crowded waiting room. When the company finally succeeded in making the connection, they paged us to a particular phone cubicle. We would all cram into a hot glass booth and shout back and forth with family members over static for four or five dollars a minute, only to get cut off before we were finished talking. We smiled when watching movies or television programs in which an angry actor would grab the phone, punch in a telephone number and immediately begin chewing out the imaginary person on the other end. We smiled because when we made local calls we would pick up the phone in the kitchen and listen to see if we had a dial tone. When we heard only the silence of a dead line, we would wait as long as necessary for a dial tone before dialing the number (yes, dial), and then make sure that our call was actually connected to the correct party before beginning the conversation.

Many countries never knew this frustration because vast sections of the world have never had the landline technology. Yet today these countries are very connected with cell phones, which leapfrogged over the technology that required telephone lines strung on wooden poles throughout the countryside. A few years ago I was standing in an indigenous community of the Ecuadorian jungle with a team from the United States. We were speaking with a shaman of that tribe and listening to him tell of the legends, animistic beliefs, fears and witchcraft that defined everyday life and religion for them. His story was made more powerful since he was dressed in traditional body paint, beads and feathers. We felt we were unearthing the deepest beliefs of some hidden tribe that time had forgotten when we suddenly heard a phone ringing. I looked around at my team as the shaman reached into his woven carrying bag and pulled out a cell phone. He looked at the number and excused himself, saying, "Sorry, I need to take this." We laughed off the shock we initially felt and realized the extensive reach of cellular technology today.

REALITIES OF TECHNOLOGY

Technology is not as much an ever-rolling stream as it is a raging river that crashes over rapids and falls around every bend. The old technology of writing letters gave way to phone calls at the company's main office, then to home phones with intermittent service, then to cell phones, then to smartphones capable of telephone communication and data management, and now to Voice Over Internet Protocol (VOIP) services that allow phone calls without a phone line and using a phone number that is a local call for friends and family in their home country. That sounds like a great blessing to missionaries living overseas and struggling to settle into a new culture. But, as is true with all technology, the blessings of its existence should not lull us into embracing it without considering the implications of its use.

I was leading a spiritual retreat for a missionary language school in another country and heard from many how many missionaries managed to stay sane during the painful trials of language school. One told me that she has one of the Internet phone services and talks with her mother about eight to ten times per day. Seeing the shocked look on my face, she explained that this was normal for her because she and her mother had talked to each other that many times during each day when she still lived in her home country. Another missionary missed being able to watch her favorite television program with her mother, which she had done when she was at home. Since she was able to get that same channel on her cable TV and had the Internet telephone service, she called her mom at the beginning of the show each week and they stayed on the phone throughout the program, sharing opinions of the show's contestants just as they had done previously.

As a parent of missionaries and their children who serve on another continent, I can certainly appreciate the importance of staying in touch and keeping lines of communication open. Our family is very close and verbal, so I appreciate these missionaries who want to stay in touch with their mothers. I imagine that it was a way to minister to Mom and ease her separation anxiety as much as anything else. But there must be parameters for such communication while new missionaries are adjusting to their new cultures. Both the missionary and family back home need to work to ensure thorough cultural adjustment. In the initial phase of missionary life it would be better to limit phone calls to special occasions only, and even those should only last as long as necessary. Emergencies are different, of course, and being in touch at such times is one of the blessings of modern communication technologies.

In the case of new missionaries, cable television itself poses a danger. I consistently recommend that they limit themselves to local programming. This will help in learning the culture, rhythm of life and language. If that seems too demanding or results in too much of a drain and discouragement in the early days of language learning, try the "Guess the News" game that one missionary used. He explained that his family watched only the local news while in language school, and the game consisted of figuring out what the news anchor was reporting. In that way, television was still a part of life, language was being learned and the family was bonding in a common activity.

Cellular Service

I am thankful for technology enabling texting, and use it regularly, but I doubt that my indigenous friends around the world would share my appreciation. However, in several countries where I have been in the last few months, I find that many of my national partners prefer to text since cell phone fees associated with texting are less than voice calls. Recently, I was in another country and spent an afternoon helping a national brother find a new apartment. One of his criteria for an acceptable apartment was the cell signal strength in the neighborhood.

Missionaries recount stories of nationals in Africa who walk for miles to get within the cell tower shadow to have service so they can make a call. This is significant for future trends and missiological planning, especially when we take into account that some of our world's largest cities started as service communities for small communities. As a mill was established for grinding grain, bakeries were started; dairies provided milk, cheese and butter; tanners took the cowhides and made leather goods; and butchers provided beef. They all needed buildings constructed and homes to live in. The process continued and resulted in the massive urban centers we know today.

Ideas and innovations have consequences. I met an anthropologist on a plane who was returning to the United States after a successful consultation for a petroleum company's Amazon basin pipeline project. His challenge was to discover why local indigenous tribes had become hostile to the plan to run a pipeline across the river in an unpopulated and isolated area of the jungle. The upriver and downriver chiefs came with their warriors and vowed trouble if the project continued. After his ethnographic research and field investigation, he was able to determine that it had little to do with the petroleum, as was suspected. Rather, the upriver and downriver chiefs knew that if a pipeline was suspended over the river it would become a natural bridge and a new community would develop there, thus weakening their respective communities. I could tell by his smile that he had resolved the issue. When I pressed to know how, he responded, "We simply put the pipeline under the river and moved on." Even the indigenous tribes in the jungle understood enough about societal development to know that anywhere people are naturally drawn (such as a waterhole), a new community will develop. The same is true of areas of stronger cell signals. These will draw people on a recurring basis and will result in the same. Field missionaries can mark and watch these areas with an eye for evangelism and church planting strategies.

The prolific growth of cell phone usage has great implications for missions. National church pastors and their members are instantly in touch with each other and their counterparts around their countries. An invitation to attend an evangelistic campaign, teaching seminar or denominational meeting was once word of mouth and only occurred when someone traveled to another part of the country. Today, it is only a call or text away. Cell phones are used for encouragement and counsel among national workers. Missionaries are also able to connect easily with one another for the same reasons.

The ubiquitous cell phone also enables missionaries to employ methods that were previously impossible. The uses of SIM cards are growing in complexity and creativity. For instance, sensitive information, messages or videos stored on SIM cards can be easily transported in creative-access locations and used to transform a cell phone into a proclaimer of the gospel message. Even though the popular use of cell phones is decades old, new generations of cell phones and smartphones yield ever more uses for spreading the gospel and discipling believers.

INTERNET

While Internet access is not yet available to the extent that missionaries may take for granted, it is increasingly connecting people and ideas around the world. An international youth ministry defends its common strategy and methods throughout many cultures with the argument that the Internet has so connected the youth culture that young people around the world hold many things in common. I regularly receive friend requests on Facebook from far-flung ministers and missionaries I would never otherwise meet.

The number and influence of bloggers have resulted in attention being drawn to political dynamics and lobbying that would have otherwise passed unnoticed. The revolutions of the Arab Spring fed off of and back into blogs, Facebook and Twitter accounts. Crimes and coverups that the populace refuses to allow governments to "overlook" are publicized through social media, resulting in front-page attention and action. Mommy bloggers are able to promote little known products by trumpeting their benefits, resulting in a tipping point of popularity, or by warning of the dangers of other products, resulting in improvements or their recall from the market. Missionaries and missiologists constantly should be exploring ways to fully utilize these technologies for evangelism, recruiting missionaries, church planting, support raising and advancing the kingdom of Christ.

When I was a child, the *Jetsons* cartoon featured telephones with television screens allowing the speakers to see each other as they talked. My friends and I laughed about how you would have to make sure you were dressed properly and combed your hair before you answered the phone. The comics page also depicted a futuristic Dick Tracy looking at and speaking into his wristwatch phone. Of course, the future has arrived. We may not have the flying cars and jetpacks we were promised, but we definitely have Skype and Apple Watches, and other new technologies coming at increasing speeds.

Communication technologies such as Skype and Google Hangouts allow missionaries to remain in touch with family members, conference chat with missionaries in distant locations to save on travel budgets, and enable missionaries to continue their education in formal and informal ways even from the field. I have checked email from isolated areas of the Andes in an Internet café running a dusty, old PC off of car batteries.

When we consider the threat from the changes that new technology brings, the tendency is to block it or hold it off as long as possible. Sometimes the dangers are real. The vast numbers of men (and many women) who are trapped in a web of porn addiction makes us want to forbid all online access at first thought. However, the beneficial uses of the Internet attest to its value, although we must maintain careful use.

Mission agencies use the Internet to recruit new candidates, communicate with field personnel and conduct banking on behalf of their internationally based workers, among many other uses. Questions and counsel that once required months are now addressed in the same hour they arise. Member care is often able to get involved when there is a need before the crisis worsens and missionaries are lost. Even matters as mundane as a mission's policies and procedures manual can be put online and tweaked as necessary, allowing constantly updated procedures that are instantly available and avoiding the costly mailing of hard copies of material to physical addresses around the world.

Mutual edification among missionaries is another benefit of the Internet. Most missionaries have a blog or a website enabling easier donations or ways to obtain prayer requests. An annual mission meeting of missionaries is a costly gathering, but it is an investment in the mental health of missionaries who can share fellowship with one another, edify the discouraged, share ministry news and pray for each other. While face-to-face interaction is irreplaceable, the Internet allows for a functional substitute and meets many of these needs on a more regular basis.

Another benefit of the Internet for missionaries is access to sound teaching for personal discipleship. I remember being on the field before the Internet, living in a city where there was no cable TV, no North American-style restaurants and nothing in English—no magazines or newspapers. I mostly lamented the absence of Christian books and my church friends for personal spiritual growth. A friend sent me a copy of J. I. Packer's *A Quest for Godliness* when it came out, and it was to me a cup of cold water in a dry and weary land. I not only read it cover to cover, I wrote almost as much in it as Dr. Packer did, recording my thoughts and personal interaction in the margins as I read. Many missionaries go to lesser developed regions of the world today. Yet the Internet offers much more to these missionaries in isolated places: Bible study resources, dictionaries, language helps and countless books in electronic format.

While the Internet can be of great benefit on the field, given their unique circumstances missionaries should take care in its use. The very isolation from others requires that missionaries exercise self-discipline in the amount of time spent online, and that mission agencies endeavor to ensure that new candidates are people who understand the dangers and are able to discipline themselves in the sites they frequent and the amount of time they spend online. Every hour on the computer is an hour lost learning the culture and local language use, building relationships with nationals, and visiting in their homes—all essential for successful missions ministries.

Just as I share this caution for missionaries, I want to also share a word of encouragement to any missionary who reads this and is convicted or challenged when evaluating how this challenge is played out in his or her life. Do not despair or allow the enemy to leave you in a state of conviction and regret. Seek the Lord for ways to make adjustments that will bear fruit in your ministry while also maintaining healthy connections with home. Remember that finding the right balance on this issue is a matter of discernment and prayer, so seek the Lord, submit to him and trust his leadership. Remember that he is good and not only desires your ministry to be fruitful but for you to have joy as you serve in it.

BENEFITS AND CHALLENGES

The benefits of technology and the advances in international travel are innumerable for the world of missiology and the practice of missions. Missionaries face fewer anxieties knowing that they can stay in touch with family and friends, sharing prayer requests and having friends who are just a few keystrokes away during times of crisis and loneliness, and that they can even return home quickly if necessary. Missionaries may communicate with supporters and prayer partners as special needs arise or monthly support levels drop. Field personnel can contact the home office when an administrative ruling is required or an exception to a policy manual rule is desired without having to wait for weeks or months to get an answer. When medical emergencies arise or a missionary family needs the intervention of member care counselors, help is as close as a cell phone. In fact, while typing this paragraph in another country, I received a text message from a friend in the United States informing me that a coworker we were praying for has just come out of surgery and doctors do not think it is cancer. The ability to connect can be a great blessing.

In addition to the methods for communication that are multiplying and increasing in velocity, there are countless missiological applications for all types of technology as it is developed. A sad reality in this fallen world is the proliferation of wars. Yet it is true that technology always advances in time of war. The medical sciences advance at increasing speed since medicines, procedures and products for treating injury and disease receive approval and testing far more quickly than they normally would in peacetime. Newer weapons and more advanced technology for waging war and destroying people and places have nations competing for first place in the race for the most firepower in the shortest time. Admittedly, no one relishes the destructive part of the race, but its result is newer methods for the business of hurting people as well as healing the victims, and these newer technologies find civilian applications. So missionaries may benefit from changes.

The US military and diplomatic corps were once at a decided disadvantage in foreign relations with many nations. The way Americans acted, reacted and interacted living among those in Southeast Asia in those days spawned the book and subsequent term *The Ugly American*.[2] Anthropologist Edward T. Hall was engaged to teach skills in intercultural communication and cultural understanding to assist our government in communicating more clearly in culturally appropriate ways. The discipline of intercultural communication that is so valuable for missionaries actually came about from the subsequent understanding of communication in international relationships. Countless missionaries have read the books that resulted from his study and application, and have been helped to be more effective communicators of the gospel in the countries where they serve.

Multinational corporations often pioneer advances in their business and marketing schemes that missionaries may find helpful in reaching the nations. For instance, technology exists for marketing firms to broadcast a commercial for a certain product using cell phones. One such scheme is called proximity marketing. This is sending a text message to all the cell phones in a certain radius announcing a new product or service and instructing interested parties to dial a certain number to obtain more information. Thinking of strategic missiological applications, a missionary wanting to reach all of the speakers of a particular language in a large urban center could use such technology to send a text message in that language to all the cell phones in the area inviting their owners to dial a certain number to hear the story of the life of Jesus. Creative minds could imagine hundreds of uses for such technology as ways to get beyond locked doors, gated communities and overprotective maids, while staying under the radar of watching eyes. In how many ways could technology help missions, and which ones go too far? Is the increasingly advanced and complex technology trend helping or hurting?

When my family and I went to the mission field we were given a flannelgraph to use for evangelism and teaching. A flannelgraph set consists of a trifold board covered with felt that can be placed on a table or be held when teaching. The set includes hundreds of felt figures representing the characters of the Bible, palm trees, camels, donkeys, sheep, tabernacle furnishings, the ark, a burning bush and so forth. The teacher arranged figures on the felt board to aid in telling Bible stories and teaching God's Word. I used the set a few times, but my wife used it repeatedly to teach the Quichua children Bible stories week by week. One missionary in our mission grudgingly accepted the flannelgraph, but was absolutely against others using a filmstrip projector. This device basically consisted of a bright bulb that projected images from a filmstrip onto a screen. The operator turned a knob on the projector to advance the story frame by frame. It was basically a slide projector in which the slides were contained on a five or six foot length of film. His argument for refusing to use such technology was that the apostle Paul never had such a device. He was deeply concerned about what a missionary would do if the power went out, which it did with regularity in those days. Most missionaries laugh when thinking of his reticence to use anything electrical in his ministry in the same way that we smile at the businessmen who were afraid to have a telephone on their desks when telephones were first available. All technology is foreign when first introduced, and it may be wiser to be cautious before diving headfirst into early adoption of technology along with the unintended shifts and transitions that it can bring.

Increasingly invasive and complex technology will not go away or always be innocuous by wishing it so any more than the sun will refrain from setting simply because we hate for the day to end. Technological change and its ongoing development are as sure as the daily setting of the sun while the Lord tarries and leaves us here. The question before us is not how we can hide from it but rather how we could use all the lawful means at our disposal to advance the kingdom and bring glory to the Lord all over his world. I recently read of a device that is available to rent for $60,000, or to purchase for $330,000, that allows the user to send a projected hologram to anywhere in the world, perhaps to multiple locations at the same time.[3] The suggested business application was presentations for training, sales or shareholder presentations to save on airline travel, food, entertaining and hotel rooms required for multinational corporations to hold such meetings at a worldwide level. I wondered about the day when technology catches up and prices fall: Might there be missionary applications? Could mission agencies use such technology for continuing education, member care or evangelism training among its members? Could missionaries use such technology for evangelizing peoples in creative-access locations, for training crowds of pastors in ways that make training more accessible to multiple language groups by dubbing their language audio onto the digital hologram, or to diverse levels on the orality-literacy continuum by sending the hologram rather than a book or a website link to read? This may seem unreal to us today, but remember that video calls were once the science of the futuristic cartoons I watched as a child. And I now communicate regularly with my family overseas through the very technology that formerly seemed impossible.

The challenges of the changes that come our way at increasing frequency and speed require that missionaries stay abreast and be aware. A consideration of the Amish communities reveals much that we could admire about living a simpler life devoid of the tyranny of today's technological demands. And yet, at the same time, we lament all that would not be available to our efforts to spread the gospel and do the work of missions if we were to reject today's technology. Rather than judge technology by our first impression of it, we should factor in the particular application of the technology that brought it to our attention. When learning that the Internet brings ready access to pornography and gambling, it is easy to judge the Internet as evil, and perhaps seek to get it out of our home. Yet a deeper investigation brings a broader understanding and shows that the Internet is also useful for Bible study, banking, communicating with church and supporters, and evangelism.

As modern technology brings new methods, the missionaries using them must factor in challenges and changes. The speed of instant communication grants the ability to ask and answer questions immediately. However, instantaneous communication is not always best. How many of us have answered an email rashly and later regretted firing off an answer in the heat of the moment when further reflection revealed the foolishness of having done so? We must manage the pace of our lives and not allow the pace of the world to manage our actions.

A new missionary on the field often will feel frustration and vulnerability due to a lack of language skills, loneliness and the loss of routines (whatever you can do without having to think about it) because even the simplest tasks like ordering at a restaurant or answering the phone require much thought, effort and usually embarrassment. The daily life of people in the new country will remain a mystery to the missionary since he or she has not learned the culture or worldview of the people. Never forget that the key to learning the culture is learning the language, and the key to learning the language is learning the culture. The only way to do either is to do both—be immersed in the culture and do so as a learner, remembering that this school is a 24/7 university that gives diplomas only to those who diligently and tirelessly apply themselves.

Today's technology seems to war against such painstaking application. When lonely, today's missionary needs only to get online at home or in an Internet café to chat with friends or read about latest events in their lives on Facebook, Twitter or blogs. When desiring to know what is going on in the world, simply peruse the news online. When frustrated with the language or some stressful cultural dynamic that makes no sense, it's easy to give up and watch episodes of a favorite television show online to decompress. When you want to know how to say some phrase in the new language, just Google it on your smartphone or text a friend to find out.

In years past, loneliness drove missionaries to make friends in the culture. A desire for human interaction required dropping by their house or visiting with them when they dropped by. When wondering what was going on in the world, they read the town newspaper or watched the local television news, developing language skills and vocabulary in the process. When wondering about some confusing aspect of local life, they asked their new local friends and cultural informants. The social and curious nature that God has built into most of us results in learning the culture, the language, the rhythm of life, the food, the transportation system, the hopes, dreams, aspirations, fears and anxieties of the people as a very natural style of living life in a new place. However, technology has a way of insulating those who are more comfortable alone and wish to remain so. It can be a shield to hide behind when faced with the hard and humbling challenge of starting from scratch in a new culture.

Technology also challenges those who would prefer to be in the culture, practicing the language, building relationships, evangelizing, planting churches and discipling among those in the new culture. More than one missionary has been frustrated by the number of hours required to read and write reports for the home office, deal with correspondence with other field missionaries, answer emails from supporting churches, and file forms for insurance, taxes or visas. It seems that the more time- and labor-saving devices and technology are developed, the less time we have to do our ministry and the harder we have to work to get caught up. Whether missionaries are online for fun or business, when their daily schedule is dominated by technology and virtual relationships they are not only unable to minister in the country as they came to do, they are sometimes perceived by those in the target culture to be disinterested in them and their lives. This may be completely untrue and an unfair assessment, but they perceive it to be true, and perception is the reality they live in.

Missionaries must set boundaries and limits. To avoid being drawn into the trap of the electronic time stealers multiplying around us, missionaries must be intentional about being in the culture and in nationals' homes. I often suggest that during language learning and cultural adaptation, watching cable television from the United States and all forms of Internet usage should be limited to no more than thirty minutes per day. Mission agencies should utilize a cultural acquisition checklist of activities to accomplish to enable missionaries to learn the language and culture. Knowing that significant progress is being made gives the missionary and the administrator confidence that the time spent in electronic retreats are not distracting from the essential tasks associated with beginning a successful missionary career.

CONCLUSION

You must leave to be able to cleave. You will never adjust to the new culture and make heart-level friends if you never leave the old culture. Even though you have finally arrived in your new culture, the hours you spend every day writing and answering emails, posting on Facebook, tweeting, Skyping and reading news in your local home paper prolong the process of getting into the new culture, language and friendships. A mission agency administrator visiting a missionary family on the field asked what the local time was. The missionary stared at her watch for a few moments, prompting him to ask if her watch was broken. She responded, "No, it's just that I am adjusting for time zone differences since I keep it on the time back home to feel connected to life there." He rightly sensed her hesitancy to leave and cleave. At the end of the day, it doesn't matter what time your watch says about the hour of the day, but rather what it says about you. Whether you prefer the distraction of technology or are merely allowing it, an adjustment needs to be made and parameters need to be set if you are going to settle in well to life and be the best intercultural missionary you can possibly be.

Technology brings with it sweeping changes in the ways we can serve the Lord in missions around the world, and we are wise to employ them for his glory. However, let us embrace technology with forethought as to ways that "how" we do missions in a particular time and circumstance can impact the "what" we are to do in missions, being careful to remember that evangelism and church planting takes place best in the context of relationships. There is no substitute for living with those we serve.

- 4 -

Short-Term Missions

G O AHEAD, I ALREADY TOLD THEM THAT," the missionary translator said to the volunteer mission team preacher. It seems he was preaching his own sermon instead of communicating what the speaker was saying. This missionary was superb in many respects, but he had little patience for short-term teams. "I don't have time to handhold people who will cause problems in our work," he would say, believing that he would have to clean up when they were gone. The number of international short-term missions (STM) teams has exploded over the last few decades, and slowly missionaries have begun to see their value. Missionaries have moved from asking whether to work with STM teams to how they can incorporate them into their ministry plan. In addition to the good that increasing numbers of STM teams are able to accomplish on the field, the STM volunteers return home better able to pray and serve as advocates for the missionary and missions.

Missionaries find that returning STM volunteers often become vital contributors on their support team after they have met the missionary and been a part of the work. Overworked missionaries who do not have time to recruit new workers may find in STM teams temporary manpower to help in their work, receive needed items from home that they bring in their suitcases and even new missionaries as God calls them to career missions service during the trip.

The ease of air travel and availability of discretionary income of many Christians facilitate the growing phenomenon of STM. In Robert Priest's massive work on STM he recounts the staggering numbers and types of ministries of STMs, estimating that at least 1.5 million volunteers participate in STM teams annually.[1] STM teams have come a long way from the caricature of mere "vacationaries." Proper orientation, field oversight, experienced missionary involvement and faithful follow-up can result in excellent experiences for everyone involved. One of the most common benefits of STMs is not for the nationals the team works with but for the team itself. Many have felt called to missions on such trips. Others return to the United States more determined to pray for missions, missionaries and the world's lost peoples. Others are more committed to give to missions and lead missions efforts in the local church. STMs are an invaluable tool for missions education.

I encounter the ubiquitous teams of one- and two-week mission trip participants in airports everywhere. With the increase in the number of STM participants, suddenly nationals have a high degree of exposure to North American believers without language skills, knowledge of the culture or an understanding of their worldview. Even more problematic is that sometimes their witness may be less than helpful, and this creates challenges for the career missionaries who are working to develop consistent presentations about the gospel and Christian behavior.

Another challenging trend has developed indirectly from the popularity of STM. Churches adopt unreached people groups, or unreached segments of people groups not engaged by missionaries, with the intention of "finishing the task" among them. STM teams from those churches travel to their adopted area several times a year endeavoring to evangelize, plant churches and disciple new believers in the people group. This model offers great hope to peoples who sit in darkness, but it's not perfect. Certainly the needs the model addresses are very real; often there is no evangelical church in these areas and no missionaries have this group on their radar screens. Yet the result of the church's STM efforts may fall short in the areas of discipleship, mentoring and long-term church health. Imagine starting a business in a country where you do not live and you only visit a few times each year for one week at a time; this gives us a picture of the challenges to effectiveness these STM teams are facing.

Churches that are able to follow through and send repeat teams to their adopted people group often express discouragement because they discover that what they began on the previous trip has fallen apart, disappeared or been taken over by cult groups. Whatever gospel good these teams are able to do is more than the people would have had if they had never gone, but the heartache is understandable when continuity, follow-up and discipleship are not possible. STM teams and strategies may offer much in the way of sheer numbers of potential "missionaries," but wise utilization demands recognition of their limitations.

THE CHANGE, THE TREND AND THE CHALLENGES

The Moravian missionaries David Brainerd and William Carey did not have to face the challenges of STMs. In their era of missions service, missionaries who went to the field normally did so for life. The phenomenon of air travel changed the way missionaries traveled to their fields in a few short decades. Once only the wealthy traveled internationally for pleasure or education; the poorer working classes traveled by air or by sea to emigrate for a new life. Now, with increasing ease and decreasing cost associated with international travel, people increasingly engage in both recreational and ministry travel. This has facilitated burgeoning numbers of STM efforts.

No doubt the realities of the twentieth-century's world wars brought greater global awareness through newspaper stories describing far-flung places and firsthand accounts of returning servicemen, resulting in a growing desire of many to see the world firsthand. As I travel the world today and stay in missions' guesthouses on traditional mission fields, I enjoy perusing the pages of their guest books. Some are a veritable roll call of heroes, with missionary greats and familiar names of missions history. Other names are unknown to me, but the many churches they represent, as pastor or mission team member, attest to the growing popularity of STMs in the last quarter of the twentieth century. This trend will only increase since STMs have now become normative, expected and virtually demanded by church members in many church missions programs.

Are STMs cost-effective and do they provide sufficient return on investment? In the early days of STM some missionaries complained about the vast amount of money wasted for church teams to go on STM trips. When you remember that 1.5 million people per year are going on STM trips, that is a lot of plane tickets, hotel rooms, visas and meals. Why spend $40,000 to send a team of ten people to Thailand for a one-week trip? Why not just send that $40,000 to a missionary in Thailand to use in the work? Very few churches have that kind of money sitting in a missions account to fully finance an STM team. Most team members finance their own trip by raising support, requesting funds from family and friends. In that way the money is made available, but it comes very clearly designated for that person to go on the mission trip to Thailand. Some bemoan the great expense of such STM trips, but others see them as opportunities to cast vision, educate sending churches and share the work of ministry with supporting partners from back home.

Missionaries who need help in areas of construction find willing hearts and skilled hands in the hard-working tradespeople who are members of their supporting churches back home and invite them to come and build homes for pastors or missionaries, schools, churches, hospitals and radio studios. Missionaries may need help canvassing residential areas to gauge responsiveness to new work, responding to natural disasters or distributing gospel literature. STMs can help by evangelizing more openly than the missionary would be permitted in restricted-access countries in the sure knowledge that they are not risking long-term visa permission. STM research teams can also help by conducting ethnographic research to obtain information on people group population numbers, thus enabling the missionary to design and employ ministry methods more efficiently. Medical or dental STMs can bridge into gospel-hostile communities and build relationships that missionaries can then follow through on with the newly won trust and friendship of community gatekeepers and decision makers.

CHALLENGES OF THIS CHANGE AND TREND

Ralph Winter warned about the amateurization of the missions force.[2] STM admittedly results in believers going short-term to mission fields without missions training or a missionary calling for serious engagement with the culture and world religions present. Their zeal for missions is commendable, but much unintentional trouble may result from zeal without knowledge. Teams that come into missions settings with no knowledge of the language often rely on nonverbal communication. Nonverbal communication is powerful, but helpful gestures in one cultural context can be vulgar in another. The absence of intercultural training and language skills can wreak havoc in a hurry. The ethnocentrism that plagues us all to one degree or another comes out when traveling to other cultures for the first time. This is perhaps most clearly illustrated by a bumper sticker I saw in Miami directed at the snowbirds who invade in massive numbers during the winter months: "We don't care how you did it up north." The "ugly American" seems to think that it is their burden in life to show the rest of the world how to do things the "right" way.

Lack of intercultural sensitivity may communicate disrespect, creating problems for the missionary who must remain behind to rebuild trust and smooth ruffled feathers.[3] Some STM team members may lack awareness of the tenets of the dominant religious worldview, teachings or the dos and taboos, resulting in unintentional offense and confusion. Others may lack a solid grounding in their own evangelical Christian doctrines and may teach or preach contrary to what the missionary has labored to instill in his or her hearers. Differing views of baptism, women in ministry, alcohol use or charismatic gifts can create confusion and doubt in the minds of the national church.

Some missionaries are concerned about the possibility of creating dependency and have been stung by good-hearted, deep-pocketed church members who only want to help. Well-meaning church groups may decide to help national pastors by paying or supplementing their salary, buying them a vehicle, paying for their education or even facilitating trips to the United States. In some situations any of these might be warranted and valid, but they may also create dependency, paralyzing the national work by creating the impression that the work can only be done with foreign funds and expertise. Such assistance may also be viewed as enticing inducements, creating desire in the eyes of other nationals to befriend the missionary to get the same advantage for their family or ministry. A bilingual national pastor in Eastern Europe had translated for teams for years, ingratiating himself to them and creating an impression of being indispensable. One STM team decided to pay his salary so that he could serve them there as a full-time national missionary, assuring them of continuity during the months between their mission trips. However, the team did not know that this pastor had similar arrangements with three other US-based STM churches, thus earning four times the salary he had earned before.

Another concern about STM trips is that they deplete the amount of funds that would otherwise be available for traditional missionaries, if not also causing deficits in the church's general budget as well. This is rarely the case. An old saying in missions consistently proves true: "The light that shines the farthest shines the brightest at home." That is true in every case I personally know. I have never heard of a church giving sacrificially to missions, either in funds or people, and suffering as a consequence. Indeed, the evangelistic zeal, fervency of prayers and church involvement of those who have participated on a mission trip tend to increase as a result of their experience.

A common pitfall for STM trip participants who return to a place they have been before is naiveté regarding missions. For instance, when someone goes on a STM trip and has a wonderful experience, with a missionary planning the team's itinerary, taking them by the elbow and guiding them to restaurants for every meal, driving them everywhere they go, and translating every conversation, it provides a stress-free experience. This allows the trip participant to relax and enjoy the new foods and friendships, which in a sense is as it should be. Returning on subsequent trips, led by the same hosts with similar agendas, often allows repeat experiences. A human tendency is to find what we are anticipating, whether it's picking back up in relationships with national friends made previously, eating favorite snack foods or revisiting a memorable restaurant. Sometimes these experiences lead to a genuine call to missions, surrendering to serve and then returning to the field as career missionaries, only to find that life on the field is not as easy when they are on their own. They learn that their previous repeated trips only reinforced what they were assuming to be reality, not teaching them new things each time. After arriving as a career missionary and having to learn the language, shop for and prepare their own meals, maneuver through congested traffic and reach beyond the well-worn path, they see the people and place with new eyes—often tear-filled.

A Balanced Perspective

The phenomenon of STMs is not slowing, indeed the trend is toward increasing growth, and the thoughtful missionary should develop strategies to utilize them effectively. Planning strategies for STMs are not only good ideas for current ministries, missionaries often find that STM team members are the best way to meet new supporters of their missionary team in finances, advocacy and prayer.

Visiting STM team members can also encourage weary national workers by their mere presence as others in the community see that foreigners hold them in high esteem. STMs can bring in training materials, Bibles and equipment that can sometimes be hard to obtain otherwise. Some missionaries in more restricted countries have utilized STM teams to bring in and even distribute evangelistic materials.

Field strategies for STMs cover a range that may include widespread evangelism, such as home-to-home campaigns, neighborhood or citywide rallies held in parks or stadiums, medical caravans in underserved areas, or construction. I have led several teams of STM students to conduct ethnographic research. We gathered field data in Buenos Aires to identify the size, location and other needed information on the Japanese population there. In Iqaluit, Nunavut, of Canada's far north, we researched the Inuit population, and again in London among peoples who have immigrated there from the Americas. In each case we were able to gather crucial demographic and ethnographic data, providing it to missionaries to incorporate in their strategies for evangelism and church planting.

STM leaders must remember that career field missionaries are the preferred model for missions and seek to support the work they do, not try to replace it. Every successful STM strategy and field activity should be leaned against the career missionary as the supporting stackpole. The career field missionary knows the language, the laws, the culture, the local evangelical efforts and the realities of challenges, weaknesses, strengths and opportunities. Career missionaries living in country also know the local believers, their testimonies and the history of other STM efforts locally. The STM strategist in a local church or mission agency should depend on their experienced wisdom and guidance. The field missionary should be fully involved throughout the STM experience, providing ministry ideas for the team, information for pre-trip orientation, assisting with the field experience and following up with the STM team after debriefing. A successful STM requires the integrative efforts of the entire team, and this includes the field missionary as a necessary component.

The ways that STM teams can be utilized are limited only by the creativity of the missionary inviting and hosting them, and much more good happens than many people realize. Team participants return with their eyes opened to the needs of the world, aware of the needs of missionaries and challenges of missionary life, connected with new friends among the national brothers and sisters, and able to pray fervently with firsthand insight.

THE MISSIONARY: PROACTIVITY AND STRATEGY

The strength of STM may be a weakness; the burgeoning number of STM teams may have the same overwhelming impact on local missionaries as information overload—that stress that many of us feel when dealing with an unrelenting email inbox dinging the arrival of new messages, more books being published in our field monthly than we can count (much less read), and the prolific blog posts and podcasts by experts in virtually every discipline. We have never had so much readily available information or this pace of growth at any time in history. One would think so much information is an abundant blessing and would enable exponential productivity, but the impact of such abundance often makes it feel more of a curse. We want someone to push the pause button occasionally so we can catch up! So it is also with STM efforts. The abundance and accelerating pace of their frequency could be a great blessing, but in the absence of a well-thought-out plan to utilize them, that reality will lead to the sheer numbers of STM volunteers overwhelming unprepared missionaries.

A strategy for struggling with this tension is to set in place the ways that STM teams can help advance the work and not allow them to become another taskmaster. Setting aside even one day to spend in creative brainstorming of ways that a STM team could help just might yield some sanity and peace, as well as a list such as: paint the sanctuary of XYZ church, roof the chapel at the seminary, dig a water well, conduct a medical caravan to build relationships in a new community, conduct evangelistic outreach, survey an area to gauge openness to the gospel, lead Bible clubs during school vacations, assist the university ministry with English language camps and take the region's church youth groups on a retreat. Then prioritize these needs, calendar them in the months that they would be most helpful and then communicate that list of needs to supporting churches.

Missionaries are able to participate more fully in the efforts of these STM teams when they know that the STM team shares common goals with them. While this is only one small example of how this could be done, the point is for field missionaries to decide what kinds of ministries they are striving to accomplish, how STM could help them, and design strategies and methods that guide all efforts toward those ends. The otherwise unbridled rush of STM teams can derail the work plan of missionaries who may go months without a team and then have four come in two months, all seeking to do the same thing in the same place. The missionaries will have their own strategies and methods for accomplishing their goals, and they should design ministry objectives and invite specific STM teams based on the who, where, when, why and how of what they know would be best in their context.

Missionaries should recruit the STM teams that come to their areas of ministry as advocates for their efforts. By very definition the STM teams are only there for a short time and will be returning home. Ask them to promote your work back home and help tell your ministry's story in their home churches and among their friends. The church or network that enabled them to come to you in the first place is obviously missions minded and may be willing to send other workers or to assist you in your ministry. Many STM team members make videos during their trips. Create a YouTube channel for your ministry and ask them to post the video on their own blog or for permission to post it on your ministry's website. Many options exist today for team members to share trip pictures online, allowing all participants to download a shot they missed and avoiding having to take forty pictures with forty cameras of the forty-person group picture. As the returning STM team shares their experience in the home church, suggest things for them to communicate that would really help to tell your story and cast vision for even more people to get involved and support what God has led you to do.

Working with STM teams allows you, as the missionary, the opportunity to get to know these team members personally, see them in action and assess their commitment, sense of calling, and fit for your team. God is able to bring people across your path through STM efforts whom he may be calling to join you on the field. Perhaps an encouraging word from you would help them be open to hear God speak. Perhaps STM team members' call is to stay in North America, but you recognize that they are like-minded believers you would love to have again on future teams. The time spent personally involved with these teams will give you the opportunity to identify those you want to continue to develop as repeat trip participants and ministry partners.

STM Team: Orientation Through Debriefing

The most effective teams are those who receive adequate prefield orientation, have intentional leadership during the trip and receive thorough debriefing upon return. Conversely, some of the most frequently voiced complaints about STM team experiences, from missionaries, nationals or the team members themselves, are usually related to a woeful lack in one or more of these areas. Spend time with them to explain the purpose of the trip, the ministry of the missionary with whom you will partner and what is expected of each of them. Explain to them some of the dos and taboos of international travel to avoid sickness as much as possible. Provide orientation of the destination's local culture to minimize the risk of unintentional offense, to represent Christ well and avoid hurting the ministry of the missionary who has invited you. Even when team members are scattered, preventing a face-to-face orientation session, Skype or FaceTime allows everyone to get the basics of the trip and meet each other.

Prefield orientation includes spiritual preparation, ensuring that every team member can share his or her testimony in a few minutes, give a gospel presentation and point others to Christ. I request that every team member is able to do this whether they plan to be doing so on the trip or not. God may grant the privilege to do so, and all team members must always be ready to give the reason for the hope that is in them. In addition, take time to make sure the team members understand what the missionary has requested the team to do, the primary objective to accomplish and what each person's role on the team is to be. I make sure that there is some aspect of the trip designed to include each team member in some way so that all will return home knowing that they made a unique contribution and saw how God could—and did—use them on the trip.

I also give an overview of the missionary and the overall ministry there, and why we have been invited to help. This not only helps them prepare spiritually and practically, it often enhances their ability to raise the financial support they need for the trip and enlist prayer supporters who will know how to pray specifically for them. Explaining what the missionary's primary ministry is may not be easy, especially when I am not completely sure myself. On more than one occasion we have arrived and found our team expected to assist a missionary in a method or strategy we were not in entire agreement with. In such cases I always encourage my team to be patient and respectful, to remember that we may not understand all that is going on in this field situation and that this missionary will have to deal with the impact of our ministry among them long after we have left. As an invited guest I never want to damage someone's ministry or hinder its well-being, whether I personally understand it or agree with it completely or not.

The universal orientation that every team should receive is to remember the danger of ethnocentrism. The idea that one's home culture is the only way, or at least the best way, is common to people in every culture. The tendency toward ethnocentrism cannot be erased or avoided altogether, but an awareness of its lurking presence will assist the team members to be patient in their judgments of others' ways. A Kikuyu proverb maintains, "The man who has never traveled thinks his mother is the best cook." Regular and wide travels may assist to dethrone this idea, but the initial tendency is to think, *They are doing it all wrong.* I warn my teams to guard against this attitude.

It is always good to encourage teams to begin keeping a journal prior to the trip, to keep entering daily entries while on the trip and then to continue doing so for a time after they return home. In addition to being a wonderful personal spiritual discipline for life, it is a helpful way to get anxieties about the trip out of your head and onto paper. Something about seeing anxieties written down on paper puts them in perspective; they do not *look* as big as they *felt* when free-floating in the mind. Perhaps there are uncertainties about finances, language barriers, safety or team makeup. Expressing concerns in a journal and praying about them enables the team member to take them to God and also to request others' prayers in very specific ways. As God answers prayers along the way, writing them allows a permanent record of how he hears and answers the prayers of his children, and how he provided at every point of concern.

The permanent record also serves our memory for names of people, places, experiences and many other aspects that at the time we are sure we will never forget, but all too soon we will need to look back in our journal for details we cannot recall. Years later we will be able to relive the challenges we felt then, recall how God answered each one and remember the details of the STM team experience to help us face similar ones that lie ahead.

The common practical suggestions for STM should be stated early and often. Do not drink the water. Do not go anywhere alone or even with others unless your team leader knows. When offered food in a home, eat it. Jesus said to eat what they set before you

(Luke 10:8). Practice praying the missionary food prayers, "Where he leads me I will follow, and what he feeds me I will swallow!" And "Lord, I'll put it down, if you'll keep it down." When out on the street with the team, it is a good idea not to eat from the sidewalk vendors or to eat any fruit that you cannot peel. In many countries you cannot flush the toilet paper, in others there is none so you must bring your own. Some prefield orientation is helpful about restrooms in the destination country for those who will be "going" abroad. Remind team members to always be flexible because the best laid plans will change daily. The missionary beatitude is "Blessed are the flexible for they will not be bent out of shape." Our missionary motto is "*Semper Gumby*, always flexible."

Well-informed and mature leadership on the field is crucial to ensure a good experience and a fruitful time of service for STM teams. I have been a part of over a hundred STM teams and learned early on about the importance of the three commandments of STM teams. First, give them a decent place to sleep. A good night of sleep can restore attitudes and outlooks as well as weary bodies. Second, give them good food. Make sure that everyone gets the necessary calories for the energy required from each day's activities; food that tastes good can make all the difference between a great trip and a miserable one. Third, keep them busy. Do not overwork your team or abuse their time, but do not factor in too much downtime either. When everyone is busy in a common task that is contributing to the goal of the week, it is amazing how focused on God's work a team can be. Conversely, when teams have time to sit around, it is amazing how quickly they can get homesick, physically sick, begin to notice the bad manners or irritating habits of others and notice a personality clash with other team members. Keep all three in proper balance—good rest, good food and a good schedule—and you can help to ensure a good experience. If one (or more) is missing or out of balance, the team's experience will start to fall apart.

Each day should begin with a team devotion, sharing experiences from the day before and prayer requests for challenges faced. As different team members have the opportunity to share a song, a devotion or a personal experience, the team bonds. Some team members will say that these morning devotion times were their favorite memories of the week.

Debriefing after the trip is very important for ensuring that each team member gets full benefit of the trip and is as necessary as the initial prefield briefing. Allowing a week or so to pass after a trip is good, but as soon as possible the team should gather for a post-trip meeting. Everyone could make some contribution to a home-cooked version of a favorite national dish. Anticipating this get-together while still on the trip gives everyone the opportunity to take back some essential ingredient, snack or canned drink to bring to that meal. This fellowship time allows everyone to share pictures, memories, favorite experiences and lingering impressions. The team leader should ask and allow every team member to share the memory that stands out the strongest, how God impressed him or her most powerfully, and what God taught the person during the week. It is always helpful to ask how they think they could have been better prepared. This may speak to something that was lacking in the prefield orientation or something that they lacked spiritually or personally before the trip. Then lead in a time asking the team members how they will build on the experience, how they can be better prepared the next time or whom they hope to take with them. Close the evening with a concert of prayer for the work they left behind and for the work God is still doing in each of their hearts. Ultimately, help the team members to learn from the experience and grow spiritually. The abstract lessons that God may have given during the trip do not automatically find concrete application without a guide. As much as is possible, identify leaders who will mentor team members in the process to make this goal a reality.

Conclusion

STM teams are growing in popularity and reality all over the world. There are STM teams who minister in powerful ways, assisting missionaries achieve their goals and teaching the STM team members more about missions than they could ever learn in a classroom. Every missionary wants to encourage that kind of fruit. Yet sadly there are STM teams growing in number and frequency who are little more than pampered groups of "vacationaries" whose lasting fruit is unintentional damage to ministries of missionaries, waste of ministry resources and offense to nationals. STM efforts will not go away simply because some missionaries had a bad experience and no longer want to participate. STM teams are coming. Missionaries should strategize and prioritize STM teams, recognizing how they can help while implementing strategies to use them. Being proactive rather than reactive helps both the missionaries and the STM team to have a positive experience with the most kingdom value.

STM team stewardship ensures that teams receive prefield orientation, sound field leadership and reflective post-trip debriefing that will wring everything possible out of the experience for the spiritual growth and maturity of the team members. Missionaries working with these teams will be able to identify those they would like to develop into regular team members, perhaps even inviting some to join them as career missionaries on the field. Missionaries should not merely acquiesce to the burgeoning presence of STM teams, trying to fit them into a corner somewhere, but should develop strategies to use them for the greatest kingdom value possible. I want to encourage missionaries reading this, however, not to see this as yet another item that can threaten to overwhelm you on the hard days. Instead, pray for the Lord to help you to see STM teams as a solution to the pressures and ministry needs.

For many years I have been burdened to help the pastors and

believers around the world who lack access to theological education, deep discipleship or pastoral training, so I recruit teams to travel overseas on STM trips to teach them.[4] We devised a nine-week intensive training that is delivered one week at a time, every four months or so, over three years. This also allows us to develop mentoring relationships with the students over the long haul in subsequent trips. Team members prepare lessons before they go; they know the cultural reality of those they will be teaching and the missionary they will be working with. They also know that even if they cannot return to us every four months, someone will, and the fruit will be harvested and preserved. A field missionary follows up and continues mentoring in the intervals when we are in the United States. The result: most of all the national brothers and sisters receive deep discipleship and biblical training that would not otherwise be available to them.

In a few short years this ministry has grown to over forty trips per year, and we recieve new invitations daily to train in still more places. This life-changing approach is effective for training the nationals, assisting the missionaries we partner with and providing missions ministry opportunities for the team members. The majority of our STM teachers are repeat team members who now see how God can use them to advance his kingdom. God changes their lives for good as he uses them to change lives of others for good.

Reaching Oral Learners

THE PASTORS IN OUR TRAINING in a Peruvian jungle setting were fascinated to hear the overview of the Old Testament. It wasn't necessarily because the teachers that week were brilliant instructors but because two of the tribes that had gathered that week did not yet have the Old Testament in their languages. Other groups in the class had complete Bibles, but they were preliterate, and as such they could not or did not read—they were primary oral learners.[1] We would not have helped these pastors by sending them back to their villages with an armload of books. Perhaps we could have given them digital audio devices to make the Bible available to them in a language they could understand, but that particular tool would not be reproducible by them for others. Would it make them dependent on the missionary for spreading the message of salvation?

Missionaries and missiologists increasingly recognize the reality of the world's oral majority, along with its inherent challenges to reaching and teaching these peoples. This refers to the approximately 70-80 percent of people in the world that are predominantly oral learners and communicators—that is, they primarily learn and communicate through oral methods, not via print media or reading.

Thus missions leaders need to think strategically about how to reach oral learners in ways that make sense for them. While the missionary's goal for every people group should be the full Bible in their language and literacy that enables believers to study it, the truth is that thousands of languages do not yet have a single word of the Bible. Moreover, teaching a class of students the skill of reading words on a page does not flip a switch in some binary fashion that transforms them into a literate culture. It takes decades for a completely preliterate culture to develop a high value for the printed page, to begin to think in abstract terms and to use linear reasoning in communication. Reading the words on a page and understanding the arguments presented are not synonymous concepts. Oral learners and highly literate peoples process information in different ways. Communication between them can be compared to a PC and a Mac interaction—both are machines that run on electricity and process information, but unless an adjustment is made, clear communication is hampered.

Missionaries use oral methods to present gospel truth in ways that their hearers can understand, remember and retell. That last word, *retell*, means that the proliferation of the latest devices is not necessarily a panacea for the world of orality. To fulfill 2 Timothy 2:2, we want our hearers to be able to continue the spread of the gospel and discipleship without being dependent on technology they cannot reproduce. Many missionaries working in oral cultures find that chronological Bible storying, the process of telling the Bible stories from creation to the cross, is an effective way to present the entire redemptive narrative to nonreaders from other worldview backgrounds. Providing this framework of information through telling Bible stories provides the gospel message in context in culturally appropriate style. But other oral culture methods that are effective include repetition, questions and answers through catechisms, and more traditional methods such as drama and songs.

Newer and smaller gadgets, digital technologies and cutting-edge multimedia resources are being envisioned and adapted for the new missionary to use when ministering in oral cultures. At first blush the prevalence and growing presence of cell phones with replaceable SIM cards, the increasing storage capacities and decreasing costs of flash drives and SD cards, lower costs of laptops and tablets, websites dedicated for oral culture peoples, blogs and podcasts have opened up a new world of possibilities. All of this coupled with opportunities provided by automated translation services and audiovisual tools give the impression that reaching the world for Christ is much more manageable. Forget the motto "The world in this generation"; we could almost be excused for shouting, "The world in this calendar year!" That is definitely a reasonable impression, but is it the reality? In order to understand the challenges and opportunities related to the oral majority, it is helpful to review where we have come from, how this movement has developed in recent decades, and some reproducibility and dependency challenges still looming on the horizon.

UNDERSTANDING LITERACY AND ORALITY

At a meeting of the Lausanne Conference for World Evangelization in Pattaya, Thailand, in 2004, an orality issues group studied the challenges of reaching and teaching the majority of the world's peoples who are not literate. The group agreed to continue meeting after the Lausanne consultation was over and has now developed into the International Orality Network (ION), currently led by David Swarr. This network consists of missionaries and agencies that have seen and struggled with the challenges of effective ministry among oral cultures. ION continually identifies new resources, methods, and missionaries to reach and disciple the oral cultures of the world.

The reality is that oral culture peoples cannot pick up a book, which they have never seen, read it and follow the author's argument, reflect on what they have read, and write a response. Since you are reading this book, following the basic thesis of each chapter and could very likely write a summary or interactive response to it, you are in the top 20-30 percent of the world's literacy scale. Most people cannot and do not read to gain needed information in their life. Instead they discuss issues with friends, listen to talk radio or watch the evening news.

Even in literate societies there are oral culture peoples blending into daily life and giving the impression that they are fully literate. A truck driver may read well enough to recognize street signs, a warehouse employee can stock shelves and fill orders, and people conduct their banking transactions but cannot easily read a chapter or a newspaper article. They do not read for pleasure or for learning new information. Unfortunately over 90 percent of all the resources for evangelism, discipleship and leadership training have been developed for people who do.[2]

Many mission agencies and missionaries have become aware of the needs of the oral culture peoples around them and are investing time and resources to bridge the gap. This development may be partially owing to their own frustrating field experiences, but primarily it is because dedicated researchers and missiologists have been gathering and sorting crucial data to reveal the challenges to reaching the unreached, and to make missionaries aware of methods for effective ministry among them. The researchers' ongoing task is difficult because of the way that many governments determine literacy. For instance, UNESCO counts 84.1 percent of the world's adult population, or 5.98 billion people, as literate.[3] That certainly seems to make the need for orality methodologies almost irrelevant. Yet the research of GMI Missiographics reveals that the key to understanding those figures is in the many interpretations of the word *literacy*:

- In some places like the United Kingdom, anyone who has *completed at least five years of schooling* is counted.

- In Jamaica and Hong Kong, amongst others, anyone who has ever *attended school* is counted as literate.

- *Some use lower ages* like Albania, where it is measured starting at *age 9* and Argentina where it is measured at *age 10*.

- In Ethiopia, similarly to many other countries, literacy is defined as *a person who is 15 and older*.

- People who self identify as literate are also counted.[4]

Moreover, the GMI findings show that the trend in orality will be a challenge for years to come since twenty million new oral learners are added each year. The importance of devising methods and training missionaries to use them effectively is startlingly clear in their conclusion, "It is estimated that even though many people may be classified as literate, *5.7 billion people* (80% of the world) are primarily oral communicators. *They prefer, rely on, and learn through oral methods.*"[5] Since the primary task of the missionary is gospel communication, it is crucial to employ oral methods that are effective and reproducible.

The energy and efforts brought to the table result in increasing options for working among these peoples. An abundance of ministry tools, audio resources, missionary networks and orality training workshops is growing for ministry to the less literate. But we must not fall into the mistake of either-or thinking that believes the simple difference between oral and literate cultures is that the former do not know how to read, and if they learned they would be in the other group.

The peoples of the world would more accurately be described as existing on an oral–literate continuum. Experts recognize as many as five different levels, from high literacy to preliteracy. The Literacy

Cooperative defines literacy levels as follows: People with level 1 literacy can locate one piece of information in a sports article. People with level 2 literacy can locate an intersection on a street map. People with level 3 literacy can write a brief letter to explain a credit card billing error. People with level 4 literacy can calculate the correct change when given prices on a menu. People with level 5 literacy can compare and summarize different approaches lawyers use during a trial.[6]

International Mission Board researcher James B. Slack has also contributed helpfully to our understanding of the literacy continuum. He describes the five levels of literacy as follows:

- "Illiterates" cannot read or write. They have never "seen" a word. In fact, the word for illiteracy in the Indonesia language is *buta huruf*, meaning "blind to letters." For oral communicators, words do not exist as letters, but as sounds related to images of events and to situations that they are seeing or experiencing.

- "Functional illiterates" have been to school but do not continue to read and write regularly after dropping out of school. Within two years, even those who have gone to school for eight years often can read only simple sentences and can no longer receive, recall or reproduce concepts, ideas, precepts, and principles through literate means. They prefer to get their information orally. Their functional level of illiteracy (as opposed to published data) determines how they learn, how they develop their values and beliefs, and how they pass along their culture, including their religious beliefs and practices.

- "Semi-literates" function in a gray transitional area between oral communication and literacy. Even though these individuals have normally gone to school up to 10 years and are classified in every country of the world as literates, they learn primarily by means of narrative presentations.

- "Literate" learners understand and handle information such as ideas, precepts, concepts, and principles by literate means. They tend to rely on printed material as an aid to recall.

- "Highly literate" learners usually have attended college and are often professionals in the liberal arts fields. They are thoroughly print-culture individuals.[7]

Taking into account the low literacy rates of the majority of the world's peoples should make us question the wisdom of missions by tract distribution. Certainly God's Word is powerful and will not return to him void, but marks on a page are not effectual gospel witnesses for people who cannot interpret them.

For peoples on the nonreading side of the continuum, simply learning to read will not erase and transform the generations of their people's history whose learning methods have shaped their culture and worldview. For instance, high literates are comfortable using syllogisms and linear-sequential logic that characterize our thinking and interaction in Western society.[8] However, such reasoning is lost on most members of an oral culture. Oral cultures prefer to learn and pass on information through stories, songs, proverbs, riddles or drama. Literacy classes introduce a new skill, but much more time is required for this new skill to transform their thinking. For instance, the US high school student who studies Mandarin as a language elective for a couple of years may learn to translate it on a page or communicate in simple conversational Mandarin, but the average student will not begin to think or dream in Mandarin. The basic skills sufficient to translate Mandarin with a dictionary and a very patient teacher do not alter the mind's reasoning patterns, worldview, personality and learning preferences of the student. In like manner, an oral learner living in an oral culture will not automatically become a fully functioning highly literate person simply by learning to read words on a page. Our growing

awareness of the oral majority among the unreached faces greater
challenges than we can meet by simply offering literacy classes in
the region's trade language and presenting the students with a Bible
in that language upon graduation.

People who have never had the opportunity to learn and whose
culture is not classified as literate fall into the category Walter Ong
refers to as *primary orality*.[9] Yet surprisingly, many on the orality
side of the continuum are in the developed West and may even have
a high school or college degree. They may have attained the ability
to read but still do not do so, preferring to live with very little interaction with literature. They make up the world of postliterate society, which Ong referred to as *secondary orality*. I once spoke on
orality during a missions conference in the United States and a man
approached me between sessions to share that he had earned a
master's degree at a well-known state university but had never read
a book in his life. He would only read the underlined, highlighted
and bold-font parts of used textbooks he obtained for his classes
and had never actually read an entire book. He disliked reading and
so he did not. He lived in a world that was largely dependent on
literacy but stayed in the oral world as much as possible.

These diverse levels of literacy that overlap and intertwine the
differing aspects of life (work, play, religion, education, etc.) must
be considered when developing tools for reaching and teaching the
peoples of the world. This is especially true since the majority of the
world's people is either of primary or secondary orality. Fur-
thermore, individuals within groups often exist at different places
on the orality-literacy spectrum.

Missionary Methods

A common, but understandable, mistake is to approach such missions challenges with a one-size-fits-all solution. The reasoning is
sound: people without the Bible must have access to it. The thinking

is that those who lack the Bible in their language simply need a translation project to receive it. Those who already have a Bible in their language but who cannot read should be taught to read. Certainly, both should be done, but the process can take decades. The problem with translation projects is that learning unwritten languages, translating the Bible, conducting traditional checks and balances, translation reviews, back translation evaluations, and teaching literacy along the way is that such methods can take up to thirty years or more. The problem with approaching every non-reading culture that already has a Bible with literacy programs is that those who receive literacy training do not always embrace literacy. Herbert Klem observed that literacy ministries in sub-Saharan Africa taught literacy in oral villages, but many groups afterwards reverted to orality, considering the novel skill of reading to be unnecessary for their cultures.[10] Simply learning the skill of reading does not change the oral worldviews, preferences, values and traditions of many cultures. We may think that they would certainly value the ability to read the Bible in their own language and this is sometimes the case, but many Bible translators have found that this is not universal. Of course we need Bible translators, Bibles in every viable language and literacy programs that will teach people of every tongue to read the Bible in their own language. But in the beginning we must minister to people as they actually are, and that is often completely preliterate and without even an alphabet in their language. Appropriate methods among oral cultures require missionaries to properly assess literacy levels and minister in ways that resonate with their hearers.

Other missionaries and missiologists began seeking a way around these challenges as technological advances opened the way. Suddenly, the rapid growth of technology made it possible to record testimonies, books of the Bible, Bible stories and even entire Bibles on media to make them available to nonreaders. In 1939 Joy Ridderhof started Gospel Recordings missions ministry for this very purpose. This was an amazing breakthrough enabling missionaries to share truth with those who had no other access to it. One of the early technologies utilized a trifold piece of plain cardboard, a thumbtack "needle" and a taped-on "spindle"—an inexpensive record player. These cardboard devices enabled missionaries to take the gospel to countless peoples, and leave them their own audio version. The missionary used a pencil to turn the record with the "thumbtack needle" in the groove, and the cardboard vibrated to provide the amplification, all without electricity. Later, the use of cassette tapes and hand-cranked tape players took the lead. As technology advanced so did gospel sharing ministries. Small devices with chip technology allowed credit card-sized devices to hold a recorded message, or larger ones to hold a complete audio Bible, that could be played over and over, operating on AC power, batteries, solar power or hand cranking.

These amazing devices seem almost antiquated now to many who are utilizing SIM cards preloaded with gospel presentations for smartphones. Some ministries have made New Testaments available on a small "stick" the size of a flash drive with earbuds, enabling nonreaders access to the Word. Many ministries have websites with audio versions of the Bible, New Testaments, books of the Bible or gospel teaching in dozens of languages that are free for download.

We live in amazing times that enable us to share gospel truth in ways that were not dreamed of just a generation ago. Certainly missionaries must harness every legitimate tool for gospel advance, yet we must keep our focus on the primary call we have been given—to make disciples. We are to teach teachers and train trainers. We are to make disciples who will in turn make disciples. If we are to do that well, we must take care to use replicable methods, resources and tools as we go. Missionaries who seek to train men and women who can continue their work in biblically faithful and culturally appropriate ways need to understand the worldviews of their hearers.

Reading a Bible aloud to oral learners does not communicate with the power of telling them the story of the Bible. Certainly we want to take great care to be biblically faithful, but we also need to be culturally appropriate. Imagine the scene around the Sea of Galilee. What if Jesus had simply read to them large portions of the Old Testament instead of teaching in parables and metaphors, as he did in the three "lost" parables in Luke 15, or stories, metaphors and similes such as, "There was a man who had two sons . . ." or "The kingdom of heaven is like . . .".

REACHING ORAL LEARNERS

Imagine a country with hundreds of unreached people groups. As we strategize to reach each one, suppose further that their language has not yet been reduced to writing, so of course there is no Bible for them. However, many of the people are marginally bilingual in both their people group's language as well as the major trade language, yet completely illiterate in any language. Missiologists and missionaries around the world report that this is the reality for many people groups. What strategies could we devise for reaching these people and discipling them so that they might have churches among them with trained pastors? Is there a way that we could reach and teach the masses of the peoples who, although illiterate, can understand the trade language?

One ingenious way that is currently being suggested utilizes digital technology in its myriad forms. Just as the lingua franca of Greek, the Roman road system and the Pax Romana enabled the gospel to spread throughout the Roman Empire in the first century, so missionaries are employing the constantly developing technological advances to advance the kingdom today. I have been in jungles, off the beaten path on trackless mountain ranges and flying at 35,000 feet watching people connect with people on the other side of the world through technology. Being a missions professor and a mission agency president brings me a lot of email from agencies developing newer, faster and cheaper ways to communicate the gospel or train the masses. However, I have been watching long enough to see that just because it is possible does not necessarily mean that these means are successful or always wise.

Think about the apps on your phone right now. If you're like me, you have many you don't use. When I learn of new apps that sound like the best thing since night baseball, I usually download them to try them out. I may explore the app and make a mental note to find a time and way to incorporate it into my life. Unfortunately, the only attention it gets is when I realize that I never use it and delete it from my phone when I'm in a decluttering mood. For example, my ministry is currently launching new efforts in several areas of Brazil, and this requires me to travel there from time to time, leading teams or attending strategy meetings. I like to be able to speak a little of the language in the countries where I travel, and in countries where I travel often I want to learn even more. I downloaded a user-friendly app to my phone for learning Brazilian Portuguese; it's one of the best language apps I have ever seen. It is designed for users to learn at their own speed and in bite-sized chunks of time. Unfortunately, this app has become just one more thing I feel guilty about, like the dust on my treadmill.

I mention the Portuguese app because learning that language is not something I am ambivalent about, and I am not skeptical about the value of the app. I value it highly and am motivated to learn as much Portuguese as I can. I wish I were completely fluent in Portuguese because that would be very helpful to my ministry and me. Even so, I have not progressed beyond chapter eight of dozens of chapters. I want to learn it, the app is accessible to me and I can handle the technology, but I have not yet learned Brazilian Portuguese. Thus, even the desire, access and familiarity with the technology do not guarantee that I will use it and benefit from it. Imagine how much more this would be true for someone from a traditional oral culture, for whom truth equals relationship plus experience. When either is lacking, they are dubious about the value of the information. Easier access afforded by technology is not necessarily embraced. Technology and devices may be used with wisdom, but they can never replace human relationships.

While there are countless MOOC courses available today, and many other less-populated online classes, students tell me that they prefer the traditional classroom to learn.[11] They would rather have the community of other learners, interaction with the professor and the accountability of the traditional educational model to learn effectively. In the day of readily accessible Internet, college students are both connected and technologically savvy. Many colleges and universities are making increasing numbers of their courses available online; some are even offering entire degree programs online. Yet high numbers of students still compete annually for admission to Yale, Harvard and MIT, not to mention the hundreds of other state and private institutions of higher learning. Indeed, students from all over the world navigate the bureaucratic maze to obtain visas, obtain grants and scholarships, borrow money from extended family members, and compete for entrance into universities in the United States and other countries every year when they could remain at home and learn online. Why would they do this when technology does not require such Herculean efforts and the withering expense to get their education and degree? The perceived value of education via Internet, personal preference and traditional learning styles do not yet favor new educational delivery systems.

Compare the technology that makes it possible for me to learn Portuguese at stoplights and between flights and the online degree options available through well-known universities with the technology that is increasingly available to reach and teach oral cultures. SIM cards and innovations based on chip technology will be helpful for evangelizing, discipling and training in oral cultures, but they are not the panacea we may hope for. There will have to be a worldview shift at a technological level before many will be ready, willing and able to receive truths that challenge their long-held religious beliefs.

It is a mistaken conclusion that the high value we place on advancing technology will be shared by others who learn of it. A new missionary arriving to conduct a literacy campaign may thrill to think of the work that awaits them. Indeed, they may imagine that as the plane taxis to the terminal, people will be gathering and shouting "Teach me to read, teach me to read." But the reality is often a lack of interest in literacy training. It should not be surprising to learn that many illiterates who have never been introduced to writing have no desire to learn to read, especially when no one in their culture has ever read or used literature to pass on important information. The task before the missionary is not simply teaching literacy, it is also sharing a high value for literacy and the many advantages of being able to read. Bible translators have related that the happiest day of their life was when they completed their Bible translation project and handed a completed Bible to the nationals. The saddest day was when they returned a few years later and found the Bibles still in the warehouse. The people had been taught to read and had the Bible, but they had never gained an appreciation for literacy.

We make the same mistake when we assume that a culture with Internet access will gather around a computer at an Internet café to participate in Bible study classes or that a community leader with a smartphone will complete the lessons that were preloaded onto the SIM card he received. Having the information available does not guarantee that it will be valued and studied. The fact that information is available and accessible does not ensure that the culture will embrace it in that form, even if they want to learn.

In my ministry of training disciples and pastors around the world, I encounter great appreciation and eager desire for continued training. We often teach all day long, and continue into the evenings, without complaint from the students. I have actually had pastors weep, begging for us to stay and continue teaching them when we have to leave. In many of these situations these people could find someone in the community who owns a computer with a CD-ROM drive, a DVD player or even Internet access, but that is not the way that they will be trained. Some of my friends in the United States have wondered why we don't simply make DVDs available or teach our classes online to save on travel costs. I remind them that countless resources are already available for free in these formats, but they are not embraced. Those who are able to use and learn from these models do so, but the majority prefers a person to teach them—someone to explain face-to-face and someone to walk down the road of life with them. Technology is a wonderful blessing and will be increasingly adopted by peoples around the world, but most still prefer the message in human form to disciple, correct, clarify and model.

IMPLICATIONS OF DEPENDENCY

Dependency is a challenge to the advance of Christianity around the world. Missionaries want to plant churches, train leaders, begin healthcare ministries, rescue orphans and feed the hungry without becoming the money machine for everything. The balance is difficult to achieve. How do missionaries bring what they know and have without the recipients becoming dependent on them for more? Traditionally this is seen when we build modern structures and provide furnishings, tractors, water wells, radio equipment, computers, or salaries to pastors and national workers. No matter what the original intentions there is never an easy way to stop providing resources or paying nationals once the process begins.

The logic of paying national workers seems wise in the beginning. Nationals can join the work only if they receive a salary to replace the one their current job provides. Paying them provides another missionary, enabling twice as much work to be done, and certainly the fledgling church cannot pay the national worker yet. Many models have been tried to wean national workers off of the mission payroll, including phasing out the salary and incrementally passing it to the national church, but I have never heard of one with a truly happy ending. It is always better not to start dependency models in the beginning.

In the years before dependency became the legitimate concern that it is today, and before there was awareness of its dangers, missionaries tended to do everything. They arrived with biblical education and administrative skills. They built houses, mission offices, churches and training schools—and held on to the keys. They also had all the money. When any national needed funds, missionaries could grant or withhold it based on their own understanding of needs and preferences. The missionaries' administration, resources and ministries were often like the center pole in a circus tent. When missionaries left, they took their center pole with them and the entire ministry tent they left behind caved in. Today's missionaries are being much more careful about ministry strategies and models, seeking to serve more as the scaffolding around a building under construction. In this way they assist nationals to do the work, training while the "construction" is ongoing, and then one day handing it off to national partners, often years before they leave.

You may wonder, why I have included this challenge in a chapter on orality and technology for oral cultures? We must not build ministries around missionaries who alone hold the keys to access God's

Word, leaving the nationals totally dependent on them. The fact that providing a Bible and literacy skills is hard and slow should not deter missionaries from keeping this as their goal. The nationals must be taught to read Bibles in their own languages whenever possible. The best way to avoid nationals' dependency on the missionary's knowledge is to teach them to teach others, as Paul commands Timothy in 2 Timothy 2:2. Having this as a goal demonstrates a desire that the national churches and believers should be delivered from debilitating dependency on the pioneer missionaries.

The story is told of an agricultural mission team that worked in an area of Africa teaching the farmers the latest crop science technologies so that they could better provide food for their community. The team reasoned that if the farmers had a tractor they could do what was needed with greater efficiency, and without one the work required was going to be extremely difficult. The team raised the money and purchased a tractor for the farmers. After a few years the agricultural missionaries returned to assess what remained of the fruit of their labors. They found the local farmers in the fields using their traditional farming tools and techniques. The surprised missionaries asked about the tractor. The farmers laughed in response, informing them that it was a rusted heap now, having run out of gas only a couple of weeks after they left. The missionaries assumed that the national pastors would be able to keep the tractor "technology" going after they left. Both the national farmers and the missionaries were so close to the goal, but very far away from success.

True success in evangelism, discipleship and theological education is achieved when new believers can understand, remember and retell what they have learned. Even the most powerful preachers will be ineffective when preaching to people who do not speak their language unless they have interpreters. The lesson for missionaries in ministry among oral cultures is to present the truth in formats they understand. For our hearers to be able to understand our message, we must be receptor oriented.

REPRODUCIBILITY

Anyone hearing Jesus tell the three "lost" parables in Luke 15 could have gone home and repeated the stories to someone who had not been present. The same cannot be said for most of our preaching styles. If our hearers can understand the message for themselves, that is partial, but not total, success if the process stops with them. We want our hearers to remember and be able to repeat the lessons they learn, only then will the biblical truth that transforms their lives continue to impact others.

The desire for and consistent effort toward reproducibility should hound every step missionaries take in ministry. While we are thankful for the devices that technology brings with increasing speed, we must remember that nationals cannot replicate them. If they have a large supply of devices, they can help distribute them. But when they have only the one they received, they are limited in sharing the truth with others. Learning in one style and teaching it in another is difficult.

Oral learners cannot reproduce the teaching style of Westerners. One of the major concerns of my students in Ecuador was that some of their Western professors simply translated their old seminary notes and taught the same truths, in the same order, with the same syllabi and books. The well-meaning professors were giving out the truth the way they had learned it. This is human nature, and in fact the ability to "translate" the material to another format is a learned skill; it is not automatic. Missionaries working with oral cultures around the world must make the effort to take the truths they are seeking to teach and shape them into a form that their hearers and learners will resonate with and be able to pass on.

One of my missionary heroes is Clarence Jones, founder of HCJB radio in Quito, Ecuador, in 1931. HCJB was the beginning effort of worldwide Christian radio. Jones believed that radio was the perfect missionary in that it could cross all barriers and never needed a furlough. (Cameron Townsend, founder of Wycliffe Bible Translators, said something similar about the Bible in the native tongue.) Ever since the 1930s, radio has been a phenomenal tool to advance the cause of Christ worldwide, and of course the Bible in the native tongue is an indisputably powerful resource for reaching and teaching the nations. Bible translations, radios, computers, iPads and thumb drives are wonderful tools to facilitate and assist missionaries among the oral cultures of the world, but they are only that, tools. They can and should be utilized by missionaries, but they can never replace missionaries.

Mission agencies should constantly monitor technological advances and then incorporate the tools that can assist them in their efforts, no matter how radical the concept. Radio broadcasts are still useful in areas where travel is difficult and people are spread out over vast areas of countryside with few population centers. Some ministries have invested in iPods, iPads, cheap PCs, flash drives, SIM cards, audio Bibles and other devices to give away, preloaded with lessons for students to study and prepare for classes.

All of us should be aware of the tools that technology provides and know how to use them for advancing the kingdom, but not become dependent on them. This is perhaps especially true for missionaries. Using specific tools strategically is wise, and virtually every format and technology is helpful for some aspect of missionary life. Yet we must recognize that not all uses of technology are fruitful; technology must be used appropriately and thoughtfully. Some technologies may be effective in some regions but fail in others. Using any technology as a one-size-fits-all tool is ineffective and often counterproductive. Remember that nothing replaces missionaries, those whom God calls, sends and guides, for impacting the nations. We should use Bibles, radios and computers, but we must not send them in our place. Jesus said, "As the Father has sent me, even so I am sending you" (John 20:21).

Helping Without Hurting

A MISSIONARY COUPLE RETURNED HOME from a drought-stricken area of Africa. They had served in a very remote area where water was delivered to them monthly. The water they received into their cistern from the delivery truck was sufficient for one month for their family, if they were very careful to use it wisely. However, since others were aware of their access to water, the taps on the door began soon after its delivery. Opening the door to see a thirsty person standing there was a regular occurrence, and they shared what they could. As the month would wear on it became harder to refuse desperately thirsty people, especially when upon closing the door they would turn to see their family seated around a dinner table with full glasses. Before the month was out, the thirsty would return holding very ill children, who likely would not live until water was available. The choice had become whether to give water to others or to keep it to have enough for their own family. This emotionally, spiritually and mentally draining experience broke them, and they ultimately had to return for some long-term counseling to address the scars they carried.

Missions-minded Christians are driven by the Great Commission to make disciples among all peoples and teach them to observe all Christ commanded, ever mindful that this includes the Great Commandment: to love God with all your heart, mind and soul and your neighbor as you love yourself (Matthew 22:36-40). Growth in personal discipleship gives Christians a longing to be like Jesus with hearts that beat and break with his. The Bible teaches that Jesus was moved with a great compassion as he lifted his eyes and saw the multitude coming out to him, because they were harassed and helpless like sheep without a shepherd. In obedience to the Great Commandment and with Christlike great compassion, many have formed mercy ministries to minister to the hurting around the world.

Biblical philosophies and strategies of missions seek to strike a balance between gospel proclamation and mercy ministries. Some mission agencies were founded to help the hurting through ministries such as orphan care, clean water campaigns, refugee ministries, feeding the hungry, medical missions and disaster relief, and therefore they continue to stress such ministries. However, others have felt led to concentrate primarily on gospel proclamation, maintaining that Jesus said that we will always have the poor and hurting among us. Indeed, in the Olivet Discourse, he said that there would be wars, earthquakes and sin until the very end. Some argue that it is therefore pointless to try to fix society's ills in any way other than proclaiming the gospel, concluding that any other effort is both temporary and inadequate. What is the balance for believers, churches and missionaries today?

The Context for Balance

Jesus clearly taught through command and example that the church is to be the salt and light of the world, so the question of *whether* believers should be active in ministry among the world's ills is not open for discussion. The question at hand is how to do so wisely and without hurting more than we are helping.

The church is facing issues today that are numerous and complex. Over two thousand people die daily of contaminated water-related diseases, about nineteen thousand children under five die daily from starvation and hunger-related issues, and over two billion people in the world live on less than two dollars per day.[1] Refugees and stateless people throughout the world need help with a multitude of daily challenges to survive.

Diseases that have challenged doctors and research scientists for years are changing, keeping doctors guessing about what the moving target is going to do next. For instance, warming global temperatures allow malaria to move into higher elevations that previously were out of range. Since people there have not been previously exposed to malaria, its effects are more severe. The World Health Organization reports,

> About 3.2 billion people—almost half of the world's population—are at risk of malaria. In 2013, there were about 198 million malaria cases . . . and an estimated 584,000 malaria deaths. . . . People living in the poorest countries are the most vulnerable to malaria. In 2013, 90% of all malaria deaths occurred in the WHO African Region, mostly among children under 5 years of age.[2]

Adequate healthcare for the world's people is not evenly distributed around the globe to address the needs of AIDS, tuberculosis, malaria, polio, smallpox and so on. Even road deaths are on the increase in developing countries. The Global Road Safety Partnership reports,

> More children died in Africa in 1998, according to the WHO, from road crashes than from the HIV/AIDS virus. . . . Road crashes kill more young adults (aged between 15 and 44 years) in Africa than malaria. . . . Road death is the second biggest killer of young men, only HIV/AIDS claims more lives.[3]

Because of disease, war, crime and other complicated issues, there are millions of orphans around the globe, and no one can doubt that the Bible commands us to care for orphans in need (James 1:27). Another of the world's woes is the scourge of slavery and human trafficking for labor, sexual exploitation and organs. Around the world the average cost of a slave is ninety dollars. Over two-thirds of the slaves are female and about half are children. In addition to the sexual exploitation, trafficking is often in the form of forced labor through deception related to job offers or debt bondage. It is estimated that there are twenty to thirty million slaves in the world. While it is obviously difficult to verify actual numbers, it is estimated that human trafficking is the third leading criminal industry today, which is estimated to earn its perpetrators thirty-two billion dollars annually, just behind drugs and arms trafficking. Human trafficking is reportedly more attractive to some criminals because certain countries still lack adequate legislation to address the crime.[4]

Even the earth itself constantly creates new challenges for its inhabitants. Changes in climate and consequences of human development are causing new global challenges. Every continent now has regions facing water shortages. China faces one of the greatest challenges in this regard, where, due to overuse, some rivers have simply disappeared. China is using water at an unsustainable rate.[5] In drier spots around the world, there is frequent intertribal, interregional unrest, and full-scale international wars have been fought over access to water. This crisis threatens to escalate in the future.

Climate change is not always to blame for squabbles related to access to water, but changes in rainfall and temperature undeniably impact agriculture in profound ways. The *New York Times* reported on the impact of continuing climate change that there are now fears that "climate change could so destabilize the world's food system as to lead to rising hunger or even mass starvation."[6] Farming methods of the world must be adjusted to compensate for climate change, such as planting earlier each year and using research data from crop sciences to develop plants that are hardier in warmer temperatures. This will depend on a marriage of science, technology and agricultural missions. Missionaries are the best choice to bring understanding and synthesis of clashing premodern, modern and postmodern worldviews, and to convince farmers used to traditional methods to embrace new and different innovations to result in the greatest quality of life.

There is no doubt that we live in a world of overwhelmingly complex challenges, many of which have come about because of changes in our world's climate. Although saddened by the reality of the foregoing facts and figures, some may be tempted to shrug them off, reasoning that we have always had such challenges and always will. Indeed these perennial challenges, although perhaps not in their precise modern manifestation, have been present in every age. Yet, instead of having a proactive strategy, we still react to these issues when they advance into our awareness. Some missionaries feel that they are always in the reactive mode, having to put out fires all the time. Wouldn't it be great to play offense for a change? Why not anticipate challenges and establish strategies to address them instead of only facing each challenge as it comes and struggling to find the right answer to a problem as if it were the first time we have seen it.

CONTEMPORARY EXAMPLES

As a missionary living in a developing country I was often approached by beggars or encountered them in the city. They knocked on my door to beg for money at dinnertime, they tapped on my car window at red lights and they sat on the sidewalks with dirty, sleeping, limp children. I was always touched, sad for the kids and their parents, and usually moved to help—by intention and design. Although this sounds cynical, there is a close connection between human trafficking and the abuse of these "sleeping" children. If you have seen such beggars while traveling in developing countries, have you ever wondered why the children are always limp and sleeping in the parent's arms? It is very often because they have used drugs or alcohol to facilitate the scheme. We saw the same people with the same or similar toddlers every day, always limp and invariably asleep.

Begging children also came to our door for money, but we would often give them food instead. Leaving our home one time, we found one of the child beggars around the corner reporting to an adult who abused them for their poor collections and sent them back to do better. I began to research the practice of using children for this begging industry and found my suspicions to be sadly true. Undoubtedly, some parents have been reduced to begging in order to support their children, and perhaps they must carry their children due to lack of anyone else to care for them. But, unfortunately, they seem to be outnumbered by the deceivers. The challenge before missionaries on a daily basis is how to help the truly hurting without hurting in our helping.

Another challenging aspect for missionaries in the face of so many needs is the reality that there is no way that they can help everyone. Who should receive their help? Which beggars should they give to? Should only the very old, the very young, the disabled or the blind be helped? Some missionaries decide that they will help everyone. Others decide that since it is a complex issue, they will not help anyone, or perhaps they will help only believers, the physically challenged or whatever filter makes sense to them for dealing with the ubiquitous beggars in their daily life. They believe that such a predetermined course of action will reduce the tension and stress of having to think and pray through every opportunity. In fact, it does not. Reading the Bible in daily quiet times, the missionary encounters Jesus teaching us to give to the one who asks, and the question becomes a quandary of whom to help and how.[7]

Planning for the Future

The issues facing us today as we minister to the hurting are too often met with indecisiveness. We need a plan for dealing with problems that we can see coming down the road. Multinational corporations and governments keep their attention on global trends and forecasts so that they do not get caught flatfooted and have to be reactionary. In highly competitive industries it is essential for them to be aware of trending developments and have strategies in place ready to go before the first domino falls. Missions efforts should be just as globally aware, anticipating ways that trends in demographics, economics, international relations, developing diseases and pandemics could be met as they fully develop rather than holding chaotic emergency cabinet meetings to address problems we could have seen coming a long way off.

Pew Research provides insightful information on the aging world population. They find that the world is getting older—and faster than the United States—and that the number of people over sixty-five will triple by 2050, when most countries will have more people over sixty-five than under fifteen. The world's population will expand to about 9.6 billion by midcentury. There will be a population shift to Africa while Asia and Europe's population will decline. Pew also predicts that India will replace China as the most populous country.[8] Aging populations will find fewer people to provide economic support for the greater numbers of the elderly. How should your mission's strategies prepare for this shift in coming decades to minister to the graying populations?

Natural resources will continue to play a vital role not only in global economies, but also in global needs. The water and food distribution crises facing the world today will only increase as climate changes and population growth continues. In *Water: The Epic Struggle for Wealth, Power and Civilization*, journalist Steven Solomon argues that water will be spoils of war in the future. He maintains that water is surpassing petroleum as the world's most necessary and scarcest natural resource. *U.S. News & World Report* is among the growing number of world watchers who see the lack of access to water as a growing trend of international concern. Those who are concerned with giving a cup of cold water in Jesus' name must be aware of these global challenges and must be prepared to responsibly address them.

The growth in crime and terrorism witnessed in recent decades will continue and create more volatile hotspots in the world. Tomorrow's wars will not be fought with conventional means. Just as guerrilla warfare tactics influenced the outcome of American's Revolutionary War and aviation's air power changed the way wars would be fought in the future, so terrorism and cyber warfare are replacing the war strategies of the two world wars and the Korean and Vietnam wars. In coming decades it will be increasingly harder for nations, and missionaries for that matter, to identify battlefronts. Due diligence for protecting, deploying, strategic retreats and advancing will require new skills, research and applications.

Diseases and lack of healthcare in many parts of the world will continue to challenge medical missions. Some missiologists have debated whether disease is a form of spiritual warfare that missions should engage or just one more result of a fallen world. Such debates are beyond the scope and purpose of this book, but both sides acknowledge that every disease is a result of sin. The question is to what degree the missions world should seek to engage it. Should we anticipate developments in disease to be prepared to meet them? Should we fund medical missionary training in universities, missionary research laboratories or pay off medical school debt for doctors, nurses and researchers who surrender to medical missions? How will missionaries be prepared to engage the ethical considerations taking the forefront of culture wars, such as gender reassignment surgery, euthanasia and harmful forms of birth control?

When considering these challenges and finding solutions for them, solutions that help without hurting, we must include certain people around the table. National believers around the world have profound knowledge of their cultural mores, norms, worldviews, dos and taboos, and culturally appropriate Christianity. Field missionaries also have knowledge of the cultures they serve, and they add their knowledge of the Bible and theology. But their mission agencies should be involved in the solution-discovery process as well. Nationals and field missionaries have a boots-on-the-ground perspective and engage the issues and dilemmas facing their people on a daily basis. Yet mission agency administrators will have to address the challenges and realities of their broader missionary force, donor base, public opinion and church relationships.

Making a commitment to help the hurting—without hurting in our helping—requires that we involve the US-based churches as well. Not only because they will be able to provide insight and perspective that the field missionary may lack, but also because many times they will be traveling to the field on STM trips. Without awareness of the missionaries' philosophy, strategy and methods, and all that has gone into deciding them, the policies and procedures may seem to lack common sense. No one should doubt that the national churches and leadership must be involved in decisions that affect them. They alone have the emic perspective of their culture, language, myths, history and overall reality that outsiders rarely attain. Local governments should be involved, consulted, respected and appreciated for coordination of new field policies and efforts to meet needs in their contexts. Above, beyond, underneath and all around, our decisions for a wise approach to helping the hurting should be God himself. The Lord who made us, and whose we are, knows best. He gives us life, abilities, desires, gifts and opportunities to do all he made us to do. We don't seek his will merely first, or perhaps last; we seek it in every step we take.

Much has been written in recent years about avoiding dependency because of its crippling effects on nationals around the world. But we must also avoid the opposite extreme of independency. The truth we should promote and model is *interdependency*. In the global church we are one body, and we all need each other. Certainly, we must help others in every way we can and in ways that do so without hurting, but we must also be willing to receive from them and respect them, recognizing the roles we are each to play in our global missions efforts.

Models and Tools to Consider

A helpful method for identifying and employing strategies to help without hurting is found in Paul G. Hiebert's critical contextualization model. He encouraged this process for missionaries seeking to establish Christianity in other cultures. He insists that missionaries must first seek to understand the culture by uncritically investigating it, withholding judgment about anything considered inferior or sinful until the missionaries understand why the nationals do what they do. A lack of understanding could cause the missionaries to forbid perfectly innocent aspects of culture, or to allow sinful elements to continue that will not be revealed to be so until completely understood. The missionaries should then study the Scriptures with the culture in mind, noticing the teachings of God's Word relative to the issue at hand. Next, with the cultural representatives in discipleship classes or Bible studies, the missionaries guide them to see their practices in light of what God's Word teaches. This realization brings them to a crisis of faith where they themselves recognize that they have unbiblical and sinful practices that must be changed. Together with these brothers and sisters the missionaries assist them to identify a culturally appropriate functional substitute to replace the sinful practice. If the missionaries had insisted on change based on initial assessments, the imported

substitute and requirement to embrace it would have been foreigners' rules, likely to be laid aside when the missionaries moved
on. However, when discipled nationals learn what the Bible teaches
and are allowed to participate in addressing their traditional cultural practices, they both know that the new substitute practice
comes from God's Word. Thus they have ownership in it.[9] A similar
model should be followed for finding ways to address areas of
hurting around the world today, allowing nationals to be a part of
the process.

An unfortunate pattern in missions history has been to throw
money at problems or for missionaries to import and manage a solution. On a trip to the highlands of Bolivia I encountered two communities of indigenous peoples squaring off for a mob fistfight. My
national pastor friend explained to me that this required fight always
occurred between rival communities at planting time. They believed
that the greater the ferocity of their fight, the more the earth goddess
would reward their desire for a good harvest at the end of the year.
All the people of both communities fought in this brawl, from young
people all the way to the elderly, both men and women. They fought
fiercely, some wearing gardening gloves and some barehanded,
knocking each other down and punching with all their might. I protested that someone could be badly hurt or even killed. He told me
that this sometimes happened, but they believed this would be an
even better sign and assurance of good fortune.

A missionary with this cultural knowledge could teach them
the gospel as well as basic crop science, the truth about the God of
all the earth, and the ways that he wants us to live. A harmony of
all these teachings could result in them making a permanent change
to nonviolence and finding even better crops to feed their families.
Following Hiebert's four-step model for critical contextualization
would bring about help for these hurting peoples in new and culturally accepted ways.

Sometimes the consequences of helping do not necessarily hurt; they are just simply not what we expected. For example, a relief agency went throughout an Andean region building three-walled outhouses in communities where the only "restrooms" were the village paths. They explained what the new outhouses were to be used for, but not why this was necessary, that is, to avoid disease. The unintended result was that all of the outhouses were used to store corn, carrots and bags of barley, since they were the only buildings built with leakproof roofs. The agency failed to teach nationals the "why" behind the solution.

The community's wisdom must also be factored into prioritizing what must be fixed first, then second and so on. In the medical field *triage* is the practice of sorting out who should be treated first among multiple victims. This can be practiced by pastors dealing with issues in the church or missionaries beginning in new communities. Since no one can address everything at once, a system must be devised to prioritize. The community's felt needs are not always the same needs we would have if we lived there—witness the Andean outhouses. Missionaries should ask the nationals to participate in the discussion in order to find culturally appropriate, economically viable and locally sustainable solutions to be suggested and implemented.

In missions history the most hopeful efforts have often met with unexpected complications and unintended consequences. When considering all of the challenges we have seen in this chapter alone, the needs are overwhelming. How do you know where to start? Many who begin meeting the needs in the best way they know are roundly criticized by others because they failed to do this or that, or because they met one need and unintentionally created another.

One such effort at helping without hurting is a business that makes and sells shoes and gives a pair away for each one sold. This model combines a for-profit business with a not-for-profit charity in an approach referred to as "doing well by doing good." Others with similar models abound. Some only employ local workers based in needy countries and pay them much more than minimum wage. Learning from the critiques leveled at higher profile "buy-one-give-one" companies allowed new companies to adjust the model, thus escaping problems and critiques others have garnered. For instance, in one case Ethiopian school kids received donated shoes while others not enrolled in school were left out. Sadly, they were not in school because they had no shoes, and the school required all children to wear shoes. In another case, some complained that donated shoes in one South American country hurt the businesses of the local microenterprise shoemakers near the shoe distribution point. Whenever unforeseen problems such as these arise, the company seeks to address them and implement new procedures to rectify the situation. It is easy to play armchair quarterback on Monday morning and criticize what others have done that did not measure up or for problems unintentionally caused. At least they are seeking a working model to benefit the hurting and rectifying inadequacies in existing policies and procedures when they are identified.

Sometimes poorly planned efforts to help cause problems not so easily resolved. After the devastating earthquake in Haiti, many NGOs raced in to help. They brought food and medical care, built housing, and established some measure of security. Everything that they sought to provide was needed and urgent. However, an unintended consequence has been noticed in the years following the disaster. The people have developed dependence on the NGOs to meet the needs that their government should be addressing. Such news is quickly met with the point that the government was not prepared to meet their needs, and perhaps in many ways is still not, so the problem continues. Some have suggested that NGOs should work through local governments, helping them to meet their peoples' needs, as a better model for future occurrences in other areas. The most well-intentioned aid sometimes hurts.

A STM college team from the United States went to minister for a week in a major urban area of South America. They met a young street boy who followed them around every day, helping where he could and loving the attention they showered on him. They had been repeatedly warned about giving gifts to anyone or stepping beyond the team boundaries for interaction with nationals without clearing it with the team leaders first. However, in some free time on the day before they left the country, some of the team decided to go across the street to a used clothing store and spend a few dollars to buy him a better shirt, a pair of pants and some shoes. The next morning when they loaded their bus for the airport, he was nowhere to be seen even though he had promised to come say goodbye. As the bus prepared to pull out of the parking lot they saw him down the street. Stopping the bus and running down to him, they found him scratched, bruised and scraped up from being badly beaten the night before. The team leader reprimanded them harshly, reminded them of the rules and explained that other street kids had beaten him during the night to steal his new clothes. They were brokenhearted, apologized and said, "But we only wanted to help him." Sometimes helping hurts others.

Other times the help is not wanted. The story is told of a water well that a ministry provided so women would not have to make the arduous two-mile trek to the river every day to fetch water for their family's cooking and cleaning. After the water well was drilled and functioning, the water was readily accessible right in the middle of the compound. However, after repeated problems with the well, the men began to suspect some sort of sabotage was occurring. Indeed it was, by the women themselves. When their opinions were finally heard, it was learned that their only time of socializing and getting away from their husbands was on the daily walk to get the water. They needed that time away from the demands of the home and for fellowship with the other women. The lesson is that when the nationals do not want help, do not force it on them.

At other times the access to water would be greatly appreciated. An Andean community where I minister several times a year was recently embroiled in a bitter conflict after another community had diverted their irrigation canal that provided water from melting snows and mountain lakes. The two communities almost went to bloody battle over the issue until one of their wiser elders negotiated a peace agreement to share the water. Even in western states in the United States there are deeply held notions of water rights. During a recent visit I learned of ditch riders who monitor water use, and that heated arguments and even fights break out if someone is caught siphoning water on days they are not entitled to do so.

The destruction from the 2006 Pangandaran tsunami resulted in many real needs among the survivors. Ministries and NGOs imported massive amounts of rice to feed the devastated people, including one country where in another region of the same country a bumper crop of rice had been harvested that year. The better course of action for ministries in that country would have been to buy locally, which is almost always best. A choice as simple as buying locally can turn helping without hurting into helping many more than just those in the target group. Ultimately, we must realize that we should not jump in to help without digging much deeper into the particular facts of that situation. The logical Western response to a situation may not be the most helpful.

What Would Jesus Do?

This chapter has pointed out some difficult realities of the world we know and something of the one we will know in coming decades. It is easy to become overwhelmed and conclude that since we cannot do everything, or may actually hurt without meaning to, perhaps it would be best to just "leave it to the experts" and do nothing. However, what would Jesus do? He said, "Give to the one who begs from you, and do not refuse the one who would borrow from you" (Matthew 5:42). Sorting it all out and knowing the beginning from the end is not our task. Our task is to meet needs among the hurting, spiritual needs and physical needs. Jesus also said, "For you always have the poor with you" (Matthew 26:11). Do not be overwhelmed by not having a plan to eradicate all global poverty. We will never accomplish that. Mother Theresa said, "If you can't feed a hundred people, then feed just one."

John the Baptist admonished his hearers to be mindful of the needs of others: "Whoever has two tunics is to share with him who has none, and whoever has food is to do likewise" (Luke 3:11). Paul gave advice on caring for needy widows: "Take care of widows who are destitute. If a widow has family members to take care of her, let them learn that religion begins at their own doorstep and that they should pay back with gratitude some of what they have received. This pleases God immensely" (1 Timothy 5:3-4 *The Message*). James said we should minister to orphans: "Religion that is pure and undefiled before God, the Father, is this: to visit orphans and widows in their affliction, and to keep oneself unstained from the world" (James 1:27). A casual reader of the Scriptures realizes that many more verses and biblical arguments could be added to the case for the church to care for the needy and hurting among us.

One strategy to help has sometimes been to bring to the United States for training the brightest and best young people among the needy, because after all, we reason, this is where they can receive the best education. This solution is very expensive, but we find money and throw it at the problem. Later, we grieve when they do not return to their home countries after graduation. Our best effort to help in that case only facilitates the brain drain. When the young people who can obtain the US visas and pass the university entrance exams do not return, the local communities are robbed of the contributions they could make.

Ministries that meet needs should promote efforts to be job makers, buying locally, beginning businesses to support the ministry, and hiring nationals and including them in business decisions. Do not establish ministries that are totally top down, handing out aid to needy, passive recipients and thereby devastating their dignity and self-esteem. After all, they have the cultural insight to suggest ways to help without hurting. Above all pray; only God has the insight to know the best ways to help without hurting.

Training and orientation are essential to avoid repeating the errors and hurts of the past. Training should be given to church groups, students in colleges and seminaries, and to missionaries in orientation programs. In a partnership with nationals our goal should be to incorporate the goals of the three-self model: being self-supporting, self-governing and self-propagating (other "selfs" might be added).[10] We have learned the hard way that exporting churches around the world, like imported potted plants, was a recipe for failure. The better way is to plant the pure seed of the gospel in the soil of the target culture and allow the Holy Spirit to grow the plant that he desires.

Nationals should be trained from the very beginning to do the work and to be the leaders of it as soon as possible. Rather than establishing everything around the missionaries (the center pole of a circus tent), missionaries should instead facilitate and assist (the scaffolding around a new building under construction). When the circus-tent-model missionaries leave, everything collapses and much hurt results. When the scaffolding missionaries leave, the work continues as it always has. That is helping without hurting.

The return of the Panama Canal is a good example of how to nationalize and hand over operations in a helpful way. The United States returned to Panama the Canal Zone and control of the locks in 1999, after almost a century of maintaining and operating it. The canal locks that were constructed over many years and at great cost enable ships to cross from the Caribbean to the Pacific Ocean without sailing around South America. The entire process is an engineering marvel that requires great skill and training to operate. When the time came for the United States to hand it over, some wondered whether the Panamanians were ready. The Panama Canal is essential for today's global trade and the United States' national security in time of war. When the time came, there were several practice handoffs. Every practice time that they handed it to the Panamanians, US authorities then took it back, with each side learning something they needed to address before the final and official transfer. Missionaries could learn from this model.

Simply handing over the keys to the Canal and walking away would not have helped the Panamanians or anyone else. Indeed great harm could have been the result. Nationalization was determined to be the necessary step, so training and equipping were put in place, supervision was provided in initial stages after the handoff was complete, and afterwards help was made available if requested. The result: the nationals are operating something they might never have been able to achieve on their own. That is the epitome of interdependency as it should be.

SIX RS FOR THE FUTURE

As we approach the myriad complex issues facing the world today, we must do so with a plan that runs throughout the DNA of our entire ministry philosophy. Six Rs can guide missionaries in decision making, prioritizing and strategizing.

Rescue. Save the child. When cultural issues weigh into a situation such as abortion, infanticide, child slavery or other life-threatening scenarios, missionaries should be as culturally sensitive as possible but save the child's life. This should be obvious in the acute, crisis moments of ministry decisions. But sometimes decisions made in boardrooms affect long-term appointments and ministry investments that can overlook unintended consequences of policies. Always save a life and rescue the child.

Relief. Provide for the hurting in times of immediate crisis. This may take the form of providing food to the hungry, potable water to those who lack it, housing for victims of manmade or natural disasters, or security when hostile forces roam the land. It could also take the form of counseling for grief, trauma or PTSD after war, terrorism or disasters. The guilt a soul struggles with may be self-imposed survivor guilt or real guilt for atrocious acts done in terrible times.

Rebuild. Help nationals to reestablish what they need for their world. After Hurricane Mitch I took a team of college students to rebuild houses in Honduras with Habitat for Humanity. We saw real needs that could not have been met in any other way and were the most pressing need of the moment. That disaster paled in comparison to the wars, tsunamis and earthquakes many nations have known since. Rebuilding can give them a corner to stand from which they can assess what to do next.

Restore. Do what is necessary to restore hope, humanity, healing and harmony. Restoration may be physical, emotional or mental. There are ways we can minister to war orphans that can bring restoration in the most uncertain time they have ever known. Rescuing victims from human trafficking is only the beginning of the needed process of restoration.

Reconcile. A passion and drive for reconciliation should run throughout everything. Our goal and consistent theme should be that people are reconciled to God; all else is simply a temporary benefit. I was tempted to list this first, because for me evangelism and gospel proclamation are always primary. Yet I also know that "A hungry stomach has no ears." Jesus ministered to the whole person in holistic ways, always seeking to reconcile them with the Father through himself. That should always be our goal too. Never less.

Redeem. The last R is something the missionary cannot do. We missionaries may only point others to him who can and does redeem. We should minister in such a way that others see in us the One who wants to redeem their souls and lives. Only when reconciliation with God through Christ in the power of the Holy Spirit has taken place, resulting in peace with God and humans, can true and lasting help be realized. Redemption is our hope for everyone, and that is the ultimate definition of helping without hurting.

Churches as Sending Agencies

THE INCREASE IN INTERNATIONAL TRAVEL that resulted in the explosion of local church engagement in missions through STM has brought about yet another trend. Rather than sending their missions candidates to traditional missionary sending agencies for appointment and deployment, churches are increasingly sending them to the field directly from the church. In essence, churches are functioning as missions sending agencies. Some proponents argue that this is the most biblical model of missions, reflecting what we see in the New Testament. Yet much has changed since the days of the New Testament. God has taught us much along the way, and this contemporary development brings with it far-reaching implications. If this trend continues, how will the future landscape of missions be changed for traditional mission agencies, and will that be a positive change?

DRIVERS OF THE CHURCH-AGENCY PHENOMENON

A number of reasons are driving the increase of churches sending their own church members as career missionaries. Most can be traced to the tightening of financial belts or missiological strategies. Some would argue that smaller missions offerings led to the changes in missions methodologies and strategy, but we will understand why the reverse is sometimes the case as we consider the shifts leading to this trend. We are not as concerned here whether the chicken or the egg came first. In other words, the issue is not whether the changes in missions agencies' strategy caused churches to change their giving, or a reduction in giving forced agencies to change their strategy. What we want to discover is the current reality and the wisest way for churches and missionaries to address missions needs.

In recent decades as many mission agencies shifted their focus from the traditional mission fields to unreached people groups (UPGs), the result was intense ethnographic research to locate all peoples who had never heard, to design strategies to make sure that they do hear, and to begin systematically deploying missionaries to target those groups. Part of this renewed emphasis was fueled by Matthew 24:14, where Jesus said, "This gospel of the kingdom will be proclaimed throughout the whole world as a testimony to all nations, and then the end will come." Some have held that this is virtually a formula for bringing about the return of Christ, and they believe that every people group, as we number them, must be reached before he can return.[1] Still others were driven to reach the unreached out of a compassion that resonates with the missions challenge that has been attributed to Oswald J. Smith: "No one has the right to hear the gospel twice, while there remains someone who has not heard it once." They simply want to rescue the perishing, as many as possible as quickly as possible. Certainly, any effort for any reason to reach the unreached springs from a godly desire, is admirable and absolutely essential if we are to obey the Great Commission.

However, along the way this emphasis on reaching the unreached resulted in the pendulum swinging too far, leading to a fallacy in reasoning about the task of missions. The task of the Great Commission and the definition of missions became "Missions equals reaching the unreached." That is most certainly a part of the Great Commission task that Christ has given, but it is only a part. He also commanded us to make disciples by "teaching them to observe everything I have commanded you." Unfortunately, the development of missions strategies resulted in missions as a two-step task: (1) reaching the unreached, and (2) teaching them to observe everything he commanded us. When this false dichotomy is allowed, we shift our mission agency's work to a prioritized to-do list. When funds get tight or personnel become few, we prioritize and determine that we will reach people now, and then when we have time and funds we will teach them to observe all Christ has commanded us. There is never enough time and funds.

The Bible does not represent this dichotomy. The Great Commission is to make disciples of all people groups, baptize them and teach them all Jesus commanded. Admittedly, this is slow and often requires missionaries to pour their entire lives and invest their whole career into a people group, language, culture and a single location.

The need for speed to reach all of the unreached drove some missiologists to redefine *reached* and to refine the role of missionaries. The result was a shift of missions funds, forces and focus from traditional mission fields to the least reached and most isolated groups in the world. Many of these UPGs are in the 10/40 window, an imaginary window on the globe from 10 degrees north of the equator to 40 degrees north of the equator, and from West Africa to East Asia. Most of the world's poor and least reached peoples live in this box. Moreover, this box is also home to the birthplace and the majority of adherents of several major world religions. It is truly a desperately needy place for gospel ministry.

The rush to focus missionaries and missions resources in these areas where Christ has never been proclaimed is admirable, but pulling human and financial resources out of the areas of the world where the task is not complete—that is, those who have come to Christ are not discipled—is not admirable. Admittedly, it is a painful decision faced by mission administrators, but with the new paradigm of missions that is defined by "missions equals reaching the unreached," it seems justified.

CHURCH AGENCY DEVELOPMENT AND EXPRESSION

To the credit of some mission agencies that were redeploying resources, they asked stateside churches to consider adopting areas that were still unchurched and undiscipled, and where no missionary had plans to go. Since many churches and their members were focused on obeying all of the Great Commission, they readily embraced the invitation.

Churches adopted unreached segments of people groups where no missionary lived and began seeking to reach them. They went on repeated mission trips to their adopted location. Churches prayed in Sunday services, prayer meetings and in Sunday school classes for their adopted fields and the nationals they had met. They hung pictures of their adopted people and previous mission trips in their hallways. Some young people prayed for their adopted people group all through their formative years and went on summer mission trips to serve them. Eventually some of these young people felt God calling them there to serve as missionaries. Excited pastors called the mission agency partner that had originally connected them only to be told that they were not appointing any missionaries to those areas. In fact, they were redeploying most of the missionaries who were already there. The pastors were sorry to hear that, but it made sense since that is why their churches were asked to adopt those areas. These pastors told the young couple the hard news that it would not be possible for them to go where God had called them with the mission agency they had supported through the years.

When the Lord would not release them from his clear missionary call, they began to talk with their pastors about going to the field through the church. As the idea gained traction and became reality, these churches decided to send and support the new missionaries directly, virtually becoming sending agencies in the process. Of course, to maintain the support that these young missionaries would need, the churches could no longer continue to support the other agencies, certainly not at the previous level.

Falling levels of donations are responsible for some of the shift in strategy. If an agency previously found it possible to send out fifty missionaries a year, even though they had twice that many applicants, reduced funding would make it possible to only send fifteen to twenty per year, even though the number of applicants remained high and rising. This actually allowed the agency much more selectivity in whom to appoint and greater control over where they go and what they do.

To some degree every agency must selectively appoint and counsel candidates in understanding their missionary call. Missionaries called to a career in mission aviation go with agencies that appoint pilots. Bible translators align with agencies that translate Bibles. Those interested in tribal work go with agencies that work in such areas. However, even agencies that traditionally allowed candidates to follow God's leading and gifting according to their understanding of their call have become more well-defined and strategic. It could be argued that their dwindling finances required them to do so or at least enabled them to, but it could also be argued that their strategic shift is the reason for their dwindling finances. The more that missionaries have to find other agencies to deploy them, the fewer resources will be available for the traditional partner mission agency, so changes are required.

Whatever the reason, for the first time in many decades churches must be creative in finding ways to get their candidates to the fields where they are called and do the work God has gifted them to do. Indeed, even the most traditional, denominationally connected churches must increasingly send missionaries directly to the field. Many agencies even applaud this, thankful that the missionary candidates who are called to places where the agencies are no longer working have found a way to get there. The result is more missionaries on the field, which is certainly reason for praise. Yet the question must be asked, is it wise for the local church to send their own missionaries, especially when each church is reinventing the wheel in the process? Or is this poor stewardship of time and resources?

WISDOM OF CHURCH AGENCIES

Ultimately, the church itself sends missionaries to the field, whether or not a mission agency facilitates that and deploys them. Potential missionaries should not apply to a mission agency and go to the field on their own without a church recommendation or pastoral endorsement. Mission agencies are not international employment agencies, so in a sense it has always been the church that sends missionaries to the field. However, every mission agency cannot do every kind of ministry in every place in the world. Missionaries typically have applied to an agency working in the field or type of service they felt called to. In this way, churches and mission agencies worked together to get God-called church members to the places of service.

There is wisdom in churches sending their own missionaries where they have painstakingly developed field ministries and sought to evangelize, disciple and plant churches in their adopted area. They are concerned that the work be brought to maturity, able to stand on its own in a biblically faithful ministry. When they realize that a specific area needs an ongoing presence beyond the one-week STM trip and that a career field missionary is the only way to ensure this, their bold commitment to send their own missionary is admirable. For some churches, sending one of their own who understands both the people of the target field and the missions goals of the home church is the wisest course of action. Simply having an appointed missionary on the field is not helpful if the missionary has significantly different ideas of ministry or missiology, and it could derail all the church in the United States has sought to establish. Likewise, a church in the United States filled with people who understand their church's goals and have learned a great deal about the target mission field is not helpful, because they do not live on the field. Sometimes the only way to accomplish what the pastoral team and congregation believe God wants them to do is to send one or more of their own members to serve as missionaries.

Churches also use STM teams in coordination with their church members who are now in place on the field as career missionaries. This can help a local church in missions education. When church members know and identify with former church members who have moved to the mission field to continue their church's ministry, they are more motivated to learn about and pray for the missionaries and their work on the field. There is also an abundant level of financial support from the local church. Family, friends, former Bible study class members and previous mission team members will work to ensure that the level of support stays high enough for the missionaries to live and minister on the field.

One of the greatest blessings of churches directly sending out church members as missionaries is that a culture of gratitude for and a high opinion of missionaries and missions develops in the church. Children grow up in their Sunday school and Vacation Bible School classes praying for church members who serve as missionaries. Church members hear their pastor using their missionaries and adopted people group in sermon illustrations and praying for them in every prayer meeting. When their missionaries come home on furlough, they concentrate their time in the home church, teaching through their stories and by their very presence what it looks like when faithful members surrender to missions. They are valued, loved, prayed for, cared for and welcomed back every time they come home. Church members of all ages give thanks for their service and learn to see missions as a valued and honorable investment of life.

Another benefit of sending church members to the mission field is that increasing numbers of churches develop a heart for the nations and have input that touches the nations. In other mission sending paradigms, churches may develop and cast vision for missions, but when a young person or couple surrenders to serve, the churches send them out and rarely ever see them again. They certainly have very little influence on their missionaries' day-to-day ministry or mission strategy on the field. However, when churches send out missionaries directly, the ministry on the mission field is virtually an extension of the church's vision and ministry. Strategies that the church leaders and mission teams have sought to employ on the field are continued. Doctrinal beliefs that are precious to the church are valued and taught clearly on the field. Discipleship and leadership training goals are maintained. The seamless continuity that occurs when a church sends their members to the field can be the wisest investment a church can make.

CHALLENGES OF CHURCH AGENCIES

It sounds like the best thing that a local church could do is to send their own church members as missionaries directly to the mission field without the involvement of any sending agency. Yet there are great challenges and dangers in abandoning the traditional mission agency. There are many dangers in the world today that most local churches are unaware of and ill-equipped to face. Turning your church into a sending agency without understanding these dangers is folly, and you may unknowingly endanger your people.

The Bible says that in the multiplicity of counselors there is safety (Proverbs 11:14) and that a strand of three cords is not easily broken (Ecclesiastes 4:12). There is great value in a network of like-minded brothers and sisters for support, prayer, assistance, encouragement and safety. Indeed, to neglect such biblical guidance without due consideration and sound reasoning is foolish. Remember that a wise person lives from God's perspective and a fool lives as if there is no God, or as if he has not spoken.

There are dangers to a lone-ranger Christianity, even in the United States. We hear sermons on Hebrews 10:25 exhorting us not to forsake the assembling of ourselves together. This wisdom is multiplied many times when we leave the familiarity of our network of friends, local church and home culture. Having other missionaries nearby to call on for comfort and counsel is a great gift from God and not to be taken lightly. Even on STM trips, team members are told not to go anywhere alone. How much more true would this be for missionaries striking out on their own in a foreign land. Churches who send their members to the field as missionaries often leave them with no other network to count on when they send them out.

In many countries the political climate is volatile, and governments rise and fall with regularity. Civil wars and unrest are more the norm than the exception in some countries. When a coup or civil war results in dissolution of the government and law and order, missionaries must have plans in place for getting out. Being a part of a mission family with other missionaries in the country ensures that help is there when it is needed. In addition, it is important to realize that once in another country, missionaries are subject to that country's laws. For instance, in some countries a car wreck with injuries results in the driver going to jail, whether it is the driver's fault or not. Having a mission with lawyers on retainer and a network of others to call on in such times is invaluable. Just knowing that others will rush to your family's side brings profound comfort when crises come.

Unfortunately missionaries must also have contingency plans in place for robberies, kidnappings and false accusations resulting in imprisonment. Incidents along those lines happen regularly to missionaries. A local church in the United States that sends a faithful member to live on the mission field with no network of other missionaries and no track record in the country is simply not equipped to face these possibilities. A responsible mission agency with a proven track record is.

Of course, sending a missionary to the field is not merely a spiritual decision. There are tax considerations. Someone must be able to advise or guide in matters of taxes for their home country as well as possible tax ramifications in the new country of residence. Additionally, the health insurance that covers a family at home usually does not cover anything overseas. Where does the local church obtain insurance for their missionaries, and are they even aware that such additional coverage is needed? The logistics of purchasing airfares at a reasonable rate, crating and shipping household belongings, and negotiating leases for housing in the new country requires some level of expertise and guidance. Many sending churches are not prepared to provide this guidance for their members.

In order to obtain a visa, some countries require that new missionaries be appointed under the auspices of a registered ministry in both the sending and receiving countries. That is, missionaries cannot simply move to a new country and remain. They must obtain a missionary or resident visa from the government, which is only granted under very specific guidelines. If the government requires missionaries to be officially connected to a ministry already registered in the country, then a church cannot legally send a member to live and serve there.

When these challenges are met and the risks duly considered, and the missionaries sent out from their home church finally arrive on the field, all may seem well. The income from the home church may be sufficient, and the mission teams may come with planned frequency and regularity. All is proceeding according to design—and then there is a change of pastors in the home church. Many missionaries have lost support during pastoral changes because the new pastor did not embrace that model of sending missionaries, or the new pastor preferred to support other missionaries and ministries. Sometimes a church needing to relocate or that enters a building program will cut back on the missions budget. Moving to another country, establishing a new home and starting a ministry while completely or heavily dependent on one church puts all the eggs in one basket.

There is great joy for missionaries who learn the language, culture and best ways to build a ministry. But such joy can turn to frustration and grief when new members on the church missions committee or deacon board begin to redirect and micromanage the field ministry. Missions committees often are untrained in missions, have never traveled to the country where their missionaries serve and may have no missions committee experience—but they micromanage the work the missionaries are doing. Serving with a mission agency avoids this danger by ensuring that their administrators have field experience and many times even advanced degrees in missions.

A CAREFUL DECISION

Before a church and missionary embrace a plan to go to the field without a mission agency, they should honestly reflect on whether they are trying to circumvent requirements or policies of a mission agency. If so, they should realize that many rules and requirements of traditional agencies are wise and necessary, even though they may seem capricious, arbitrary or draconian. Mission agencies with decades of experience have seen the unnecessary and unfortunate experiences of others and have put rules in place to prevent future suffering. Interestingly, I have seen that some churches who react against the rules and decide to begin their own missions effort eventually put similar rules in place themselves.

A bigger question for the kingdom value of missionaries' lives and the church's missions investment has to do with missiology. How will untrained missionaries, with untrained home church leadership, conduct biblically faithful and culturally sensitive ministry when they arrive on the field? What is the philosophy, strategy or methodology of the missions effort? What we think influences what we do, and these matters need to be thought through. Someone who has been down the road before can help us avoid stepping in potholes that we may not see until it is too late.

New missionaries should be as well-grounded as possible in theology, biblical studies, the history of missions, worldview issues, skills in intercultural communication and methods of evangelism and church planting. For instance, some missionaries use the Koran to evangelize in an approach called the "Camel method." Do you agree with this? Is it wise or dangerous? What about the "insider movement" and the C5 approach to evangelism among Muslims? Is it legitimate to merely seek to get nationals to pray a sinner's prayer in evangelistic encounters? Should we seek to preach Christ primarily where no one has ever heard, or seek to bring in the harvest and preserve the fruit where people are responding? What are the essential elements that must be present for a gathering of people to be considered a church? Who is qualified to lead a church? Where is the balance of ministering to the physical needs in ministries to the "least of these" and simply proclaiming the gospel message? Seasoned veterans with years of field experience can guide missionaries who know nothing of these things. Well-developed field strategies and methods are one of the blessings of being part of a mission agency team with a proven track record and experienced leadership. Many sending churches will struggle to provide this same level of experience and counsel on field-specific issues.

When a local church decides to send their own missionaries, will it provide the entire support package for the missionaries? Will this include salary, airfares for the family to and from the field, outfitting allowance on the field, health and life insurance, retirement, children's education, and visas? If not, and other churches or people are asked to join in, are others in essence paying the salary for one of the ministers of the sending church?

Some churches realize the tension of this predicament and instead opt to facilitate their members getting to the field as missionaries, but do not pay the full package or require exclusive rights to their ministry. Such churches simply would like to benefit in some way, knowing that the missionaries they help to send understand their goals. Still there are stewardship issues to face if a church sends a missionary. Is the church sure they are being a good steward of funds by sending the missionary, and are they ready to provide the guidance they need?

One of the important decisions to be made is how to learn the language. Mission agencies have learned through experience the best ways to get the necessary training. Missionaries may be so eager to get to the field that language school seems an extravagance or an unnecessary delay, especially when a tutor in the target country seems just as good. Should the sending church require missionaries to have some kind of theological, biblical or crosscultural training prior to deployment? Some missionaries will be in situations where either renting or buying a home is possible. Which is best in that particular context? Missionaries will have to educate their kids, so they wonder about home schooling, national schools, boarding schools or an international missionary kids school. All have their advantages and disadvantages, and of course some options are cost prohibitive. Some would facilitate greater ministry involvement, but would be too emotionally draining. Informed counsel to help missionaries make this decision is crucial. Would a local church in the United States be prepared to guide them in this?

Another danger of the growing trend of local churches sending their own missionaries is one of accountability. Even the most sincere and passionate God-called missionary goes through culture shock. There is always the tendency to retreat into a shell to create a comfort zone. Initially, the missionary may think that this will only be for periodic recharging of his or her batteries, but it can easily become a pattern and lifestyle. Some well-intentioned missionaries have gone through culture shock, created a comfort zone that required little interaction with the community, developed crutches for surviving in the culture, and resorted to essentially being US expats who simply live in another country and receive missionary support. They may go to church, but never start one. Mission agencies have mechanisms in place to safeguard against this and can recognize the pattern when it begins to develop.

Who will be able to provide oversight for your field missionaries to discern whether wise stewardship of funds is taking place? Certainly these missionaries are church members and people that you love, but they also are fallen. We want to trust our missionaries with mission funds and ministries, but as the Russian proverb made famous by President Ronald Reagan states: "Trust but verify." We may require an accounting of funds and time, but an agency with field experience will know how to interpret the data submitted.

Proactive Response

Before they launch out into uncharted waters, churches that desire to continue their ministries on fields where traditional mission agency partners are leaving should consider new missions partners who share their vision. They should ask around and search the Internet for potential partner mission agencies who would be willing to network with them to continue and develop their work. Other agencies may be very pleased to receive missionary candidates from a church and get them set up where they may serve. Moreover, these partner agencies can assist a church to make sure its missionary has coverage for the risks discussed earlier.

When considering a strategy for your church as it sends missionaries to the field, look within the church membership and identify the passions, gifts, skills and resources that are already present in your church. Perhaps there is a local population of people from the culture you are working with internationally, or even a near-neighbor culture. They could assist in language learning for your missionaries prior to deployment as well as for orientation of mission teams to have some of the language before traveling. Your church has much more to offer than simply the candidate.

Many churches are concerned about the current trend of traditional mission agencies leaving the harvest fields for the search fields in the 10/40 Window. These concerned churches believe that Jesus did not command us to finish the Great Commission, but to be faithful to it—all of it. These churches do not fault those who are called to reach the lesser reached, but they also want to teach those who have been reached all that Jesus has commanded. If traditional mission agencies are likewise concerned about the growing trend of local churches becoming their own sending agencies, could that be slowed if traditional agencies showed greater balance by continuing a strong presence in the harvest fields?

God calls men and women to missions, guides them to the places he wants them to serve, and gifts them with all that they will need to obey his call. When anyone usurps God's role, trouble begins. The key to churches and traditional mission agencies continuing to work together is for these agencies to help missionary candidates go where God calls them and do what God has guided and gifted them to do. There must be a greater emphasis on facilitating the fulfillment of God's call, not substituting it with the agency's call.

When the Holy Spirit leads an individual to surrender to missions, we should celebrate that. We need to allow the Holy Spirit to lead, trust that the candidate has discerned wisely and support the missionary until the missionary demonstrates otherwise. Pushback sometimes arises when an agency has a strategy to deploy all new missionaries to a particular place, but candidates feel called elsewhere. Agencies may fear that allowing everyone to go where they want and to do what they believe God has led them to do would result in everyone going to some location where they are not needed. Instead, we should trust that the Holy Spirit knows exactly what he is doing in the calling and gifting of missionaries. Suppose the Spirit does indeed call and guide the entire new crop of missionaries to the same place, and it is a place the agency has determined to leave as already "reached." What if the Holy Spirit is about to pour himself out there in an awakening, and hundreds of trained Christian workers need to be in place for this harvest? Let us further suppose that the places we are trying to get into with creative-access ministries, and where we want to send our new crop of missionaries, are places that the newly trained believers in the "reached" country could get into with relative ease? What if all our missionaries would be strategically placed to bring in the harvest, disciple believers, train them for going out as crosscultural workers, and then help them get where God calls and guides them? Might that be our most creative access of all? Only he knows!

Churches are sending their members directly to the field and bypassing traditional mission agencies with increasing frequency. There is wisdom and folly in this trend. There is also middle ground. Other partner mission agencies would be willing to join with churches to help them get their people to the field and provide the infrastructure they need. The great need is for churches to get their people to the places they are called and guided to serve, whatever it takes. If the traditional mission agencies that have specific deployment strategies would revert to that model, the finances would flow as in prior days to make it possible to do both.

Churches with a missions vision to evangelize, disciple, plant churches and train leaders on the mission field are seeking ways to place their people on the field as God calls them. Missions candidates are seeking ways to get to the fields where God has called them and do what God has equipped them to do. National believers increasingly see the needs and scour the Internet for like-minded ministries to come and minister among them—especially since many traditional sending agencies have pulled out and redeployed in other areas. Reaching & Teaching International Ministries is an example of a partner agency ready to help churches, missionary candidates and nationals. Missionaries serving in a growing number of countries and sent by churches desiring mission agency covering, missiological counsel and oversight are joining common passions with national believers, sending churches, traditional sending agencies and missionaries already in the field to see the nations won to Christ and taught to obey all he commanded, worshiping in biblically sound churches with qualified and trained leaders.

Business as Mission

C HAD IS AN ACCOUNTANT AND WORKS for a petroleum company that has an international presence. When the company needed an experienced accountant to audit the books and train national workers overseas, he volunteered and accepted a two-year assignment in a Middle Eastern country. Being a believer, he sought out, befriended and assisted local expatriate Christian workers in their missions work during his time there. The missionaries were thankful to have his friendship and the extra help, and Chad was blessed to be able to be a part of a missionary team. Some might call Chad an unintentional missionary.

Anna knew that God had called her to East Asia to serve in missions, but missionary visas were out of the question in the country where she longed to serve. She considered seeking appointment with a mission agency and raising support, but then decided to request a transfer from the multinational corporation where she had worked for years. It turned out that she not only got the transfer but also a bonus with the company's appreciation for her willingness to take an overseas assignment. She spends as much time as possible building relationships, sharing the gospel and discipling those she has led to the Lord. Aside from the company career boost, the cultural learning experience and the freedom that a good salary with benefits provides, she is able to serve in a creative-access country with a built-in reason to be there.

Business as mission (BAM) strategies are vitally important for reaching and teaching the unreached and undiscipled peoples of the world, and missionaries must be prepared with essential skills and credentials to meet international needs in the coming decades. BAM strategies have surged in necessity and popularity in recent decades and continue to grow around the world. Geopolitical realities surrounding the United States' relationship with other countries continue to present challenges to US citizens who are seeking to live and serve outside its borders. In recent decades missionaries have sought creative access for legitimate visas that enable them to live and serve in countries closing their borders to traditional missionaries.

However, BAM has been controversial in certain cases where missionaries gained access to a country by connecting with a shell company that only existed for the purpose of facilitating legal residency for missionaries in a closed country, allowing missionaries to merely pretend to be involved in business. Such activity was questioned as unethical and not appropriate for Christian missionaries. Other missionaries deployed with a BAM model and actually engaged to some degree in the careers they list on their visa forms. Their specific level of involvement resulted in a ministry with more or less integrity as well as providing networks of relationships within the community. The need for creative-access platforms and the financial support that BAM provides demands that future missionaries obtain skills and credentials that will be seen as valuable to governments and immigration authorities where they hope to serve. Just as secular university students give serious consideration to job availability and the relative earning power of various careers when choosing their college major, so future missionaries should study their options and choose wisely. This chapter will consider the need for BAM, ethical concerns, trends informing the future opportunities and reflect on helpful training for future missionaries.

THE NEED

The BAM trend grew out of the need for both creative access and income; it is as old as the Bible, but as current as today's newspaper.[1] The trend is receiving much attention in the form of journal articles, books, training events and unprecedented missiological strategies. Indeed, one missionary describes himself as a provider of "landing pads." He travels to creative-access countries to form small companies that will hire Christian workers, thus obtaining their visas, guaranteeing legal residence and a platform for ministry. Entire books and academic research dissertations have been written in recent years that plumb the depths of BAM and explain the myriad creative-access platforms. Rather than repeat the excellent work to date explaining and presenting BAM, I want to reflect on the philosophical idea, ethical concerns, global need for and future of BAM and creative-access platforms in missions.

WORKING WITHOUT PERMISSION

The apostle Paul's work of making tents with Priscilla and Aquila is considered a kind of BAM, appropriately called "tentmaking," which focused on providing his support when necessary. However the aspect of BAM strategy that has seen such a steep climb in popularity in recent decades focuses more on getting missionaries into countries that otherwise would be closed to them. Using creative access for Christian missions has not always been the model everyone practiced. For instance, a Christian missionary and colporteur named Francisco Penzotti attempted to enter Ecuador with a shipment of Bibles in 1882, a time when Roman Catholicism reigned and Protestant Bibles were unwelcome. The Uruguayan evangelical carpenter turned preacher and Bible smuggler tried to get boxes of Bibles past the customs inspector in the port city of Guayaquil. Richard Reichert recorded, "One of the customs inspectors declared defiantly, 'As long as Mount Chimborazo stands, these books will never enter Ecuador.' Yet, despite the boast, that very shipment of Bibles came through."[2] Penzotti was quite open about his intentions even though the government was against such activity.

Another successful Bible smuggler is Andrew van der Bijl, better known as Brother Andrew, founder of Open Doors and author of *God's Smuggler*. Related to his ministry smuggling Bibles into the countries of the communist Soviet Union, Brother Andrew is often quoted as saying, "There is no country closed to the Gospel. Anyone can get in—not everyone gets out—but anyone, willing, can get in."[3] Brother Andrew's life and example inspired thousands of believers. Some joined him in his efforts to advance Christianity during the Cold War years, and others prayed for the salvation of Soviet leaders in the Communist Party and for the gospel to go forth.

Both Francisco Penzotti and Brother Andrew understood the truth that Jesus Christ taught in the Great Commission, "*All* authority in heaven and on earth has been given to me" (Matthew 28:18). The Great Commission that propels missionaries to the nations begins with the declaration that all authority belongs to Christ and emphasizes this as foundational. Without this essential truth there would have been no hope of gospel success for the eleven who heard him give it or for the millions who have lived since. All authority has been given to King Jesus, "Go therefore and make disciples of all nations, baptizing them in the name of the Father and of the Son and of the Holy Spirit, teaching them to observe all that I have commanded you. And behold, I am with you always, to the end of the age" (Matthew 28:19-20). The one with all authority has commanded us to obey this commission. While there are many authorities who will oppose this work, their authority pales in comparison to the ultimate authority who will be with us in our obedience until the very end.

Penzotti and Brother Andrew are merely two representatives of the thousands of missionaries through the years, in the line of Peter and John, who obeyed Jesus no matter what the local authorities said (Acts 4:15-21). Certainly, the Bible contains clear instructions about obeying the government, such as Romans 13:1-5:

> Let every person be subject to the governing authorities. For there is no authority except from God, and those that exist have been instituted by God. Therefore whoever resists the authorities resists what God has appointed, and those who resist will incur judgment. For rulers are not a terror to good conduct, but to bad. Would you have no fear of the one who is in authority? Then do what is good, and you will receive his approval, for he is God's servant for your good. But if you do wrong, be afraid, for he does not bear the sword in vain. For he is the servant of God, an avenger who carries out God's wrath on the wrongdoer. Therefore one must be in subjection, not only to avoid God's wrath but also for the sake of conscience.

And 1 Timothy 2:1-3:

> First of all, then, I urge that supplications, prayers, intercessions, and thanksgivings be made for all people, for kings and all who are in high positions, that we may lead a peaceful and quiet life, godly and dignified in every way. This is good, and it is pleasing in the sight of God our Savior.

Yet the government is to be in submission to God. To the degree that a government forbids what God has clearly commanded or commands what God has clearly forbidden, we must obey God rather than the government.

In their efforts to obey the Great Commission some, such as Penzotti and Brother Andrew, have simply forged ahead and sought to obey the call and commission Jesus gave his church, even when it was illegal or dangerous to do so. Among them we number the martyrs who fill the ranks of the faithful witnesses who ventured all in the face of outrageous opposition. Others have found it preferable to use creative-access platforms to reach and teach the nations of the world, arguing that the better course of wisdom is to be as wise as serpents but harmless as doves in the advance of the kingdom, and that to live longer to witness more prolifically is wiser than dying an unnecessarily early death. Each has his or her own call and leadership from God, and we should respect and appreciate every believer who seeks to be faithful to him who calls.

One of the ways to enter legally and serve among the nations that are increasingly closing their doors to traditional missionaries is through the BAM creative-access platform strategy. Missionaries who enter countries on work visas have been able to fly under the radar of watchful eyes that seek to filter out Christian workers with evangelistic intentions to convert the lost, plant churches, disciple believers and train leadership. An immigrant with a work visa to be an English teacher, business owner or tourism company operator does not seem as threatening as a Christian missionary.

Negative press garnered decades ago by missionaries allegedly cooperating with US intelligence forces, the ugly American image, missionaries depicted in James Michener's *Hawaii*, abusive Western-based profit-grabbing multinational corporations, and even some US foreign policies have not helped missionaries receive the welcome they once enjoyed around the world. The increasing polarization of Christianity and Islam since 9/11 has resulted in even greater scrutiny of US citizens living abroad. Many have found it helpful to possess a skill and experience backed by appropriate educational credentials when requesting a visa to enter and live in a country that would otherwise block entrance to a Western missionary.

Hearing the gospel and being born again are essential to eternal salvation. The gospel must be preached, believed, embraced and lived out in every country, and so obtaining permission to enter and live out a Christian witness to advance the gospel is reason enough to embrace and promote BAM strategies. The trend of denying missionary visas is alarming. Even countries in Latin America, long considered to be places of easy access, are tightening requirements for obtaining missionary visas. Former International Mission Board president Jerry Rankin stated in 2012, "Recent research reveals that over the last decade an average of three countries a year close their doors to Christian missionaries."[4] Clearly we face a growing challenge.

Tentmakers

Not all who go into missions through BAM are seeking creative access; some are earning their living in a way and place that enables them to serve the Lord. In the same way that a bivocational pastor works a daily secular job as a carpenter, salesperson or teacher, but serves the church several evenings a week and weekends, so some missionaries seek to use their career to advance the kingdom. Some intentionally seek an international transfer in their corporate career in order to help the missionaries in another country, evangelize coworkers and be a witness in every way they can. Patrick Lai has written what has become a standard resource for understanding this aspect of BAM. In *Tentmaking*, he very helpfully described this trend in the early days of its recent rise in popularity by listing five different levels of tentmakers. He devised and employed a T1-T5 scale to help explain the phenomenon.[5]

T1 tentmakers are those who seek an international transfer in their employment to learn another culture or language, to travel or to advance their careers, but who also love the Lord and want to serve him wherever they are. They are believers but are not necessarily called to missions. A friend of mine worked for a company that offered him a transfer to a Middle Eastern country. He eagerly accepted the offer, both for the salary increase and the opportunity to live and work in a country that was closed to traditional missionaries. He contacted me to find out how he could work with low-profile missionaries who were working there for advancing the kingdom of Christ.

T2 tentmakers feel called to missions and are intentionally taking jobs in secular fields and international locations to fulfill their missionary call. Lai considers Aquila and Priscilla in this level. For example, a former student of mine works for Apple and planned to request a job opportunity in a creative-access country specifically to facilitate the mission work she felt called to.

T3 tentmakers feel called to missions and work internationally for gospel purposes, but friends, family and other supporters back home provide some of their income. They may have an arrangement with an employer who understands their mission and seeks to facilitate it. Lai considers the apostle Paul to be a T3 missionary tentmaker. There is one chain of US-based restaurants that I think would be the perfect solution for people in this level. The business is run with a predominantly Christian ethic and worldview. A franchise could be established in a creative-access country with Christian workers, who would work in the restaurant a certain number of hours per week, thus legitimizing any visa requirement. They could be given maximum flexibility in scheduling, knowing that these employees are also aligned with a mission organization and part of their income comes through their support team.

T4 tentmakers are neither businesspeople nor traditional missionaries. They variously serve a nongovernmental organization (NGO), volunteer for a relief agency or are otherwise connected with a nonprofit organization. Since this category includes those who care for the sick or give relief to the oppressed but are not clearly and openly missionaries, Lai considers the apostle Peter in this category. After the tsunami in Southeast Asia there was an open door for organizations who could provide housing, medical care, clean water, community development and other kinds of assistance. That is also true in most other areas affected by drought, war or natural disasters, such as Haiti after the devastating earthquake that left over 200,000 people dead. But the difference is that the tsunami hit in a region of the world where Christian missionaries had not been welcome. The open door to international NGOs allowed Christian workers to gain access that would have been virtually impossible otherwise.

T5 tentmakers are missionaries with the covering of work visas provided by either an employer who understands that they will not be working in the business or a shell company that is not a profit-making endeavor. Their descriptions of a career in a multinational corporation and intentions to work in the new country listed on their visa applications are pure fiction. T5s are undercover missionaries and usually have theological or missiological training rather than the kind of job training or educational credentials expected in the purported business.

THE PERFECT ANSWER?

At first glance, some level of tentmaking seems like the perfect avenue for those called to missions when we consider all the hurdles to get to the mission field, especially for the independent thinkers. There will be no mission agency to answer to and no other philosophy, strategy or missions methodologies than their own ideas. They can live internationally, making good money with multinational corporations—which tend to reward those who accept overseas posts. There are no visa hassles, no need to raise support in churches, no prayer letters to write and no mission team supervisors. Yet, though it may appear to be the perfect answer, it is often found to be not quite so.

Consider the average employee where you currently live, working forty or more hours a week and stressed about finding enough time to mow the lawn, get the car serviced, buy groceries and a host of other responsibilities. Those who serve in some capacity in the church, such as teaching Sunday school, barely have time to prepare. Life on the mission field is no different, indeed it is worse. In many contexts, fruits and vegetables must be washed in a bleach solution to kill parasites, food must be cooked from scratch, and life is harder, takes more time and leaves one drained at the end of the day. The fantasy of the dream life overseas working a full-time job and having time and energy to also be a self-styled missionary is illusory. Tentmaking offers options to consider, but it is not the one-size-fits-all fix.

ETHICAL CONSIDERATIONS

While some churches and individuals may feel squeamish about the legitimacy of breaking a country's laws that forbid Christian missionary work, most Christians understand that Christ's Great Commission supersedes human laws. More common are the missionaries who struggle with the ethics of lying and pretending to be something they are not. *Lying* may seem a harsh word to use when it is a creative cover for Christian ministry. Yet missionaries report struggling with being dishonest for Jesus' sake. They must live with the constant strain of making sure that their friends and families, including their own children, do not divulge what they actually are doing in the country. They devise a short, tenable statement that explains their presence in the country, "I am an English teacher, a tour agency operator, a restaurant owner or a business consultant." This dodges some questions and casual inquiries, but when a friend, neighbor or police officer asks harder questions about the source of their income or asks very directly whether the person is a missionary, the short, tenable statement breaks down.

Missionaries have justified the subterfuge and strain with the argument of the greater good, deciding that getting in and staying in to be able to minister is more important than telling the whole truth and getting kicked out. After all, the target culture needs to hear the gospel and will be eternally lost without it. It is reasoned that if the new believers in the target country do discover the truth, they will understand and support the cover story. Unfortunately, many do not. It is easy to understand their confusion when we think about it. That would be tantamount to learning on your wedding night that the person you dated and married is not really who you were led to believe. No one would then shrug and say, "Oh well, we are married now and I love him (or her), so it doesn't matter." No, the offense and resulting suspicion would make you wonder what else is not true, who this person really is and whether you can trust anything he or she says.

Even among BAM missionaries, both those who are involved in it for creative access and those who need the income, there are diverse levels of BAM and full disclosure. Those who list jobs for visa covering in the country can be said to fall into the category of job takers, job fakers or job makers. When a US citizen takes a job teaching at an international university, he or she may be taking the job and income from a qualified national. In other cases, nationals easily recognize fakers who are not actually working in the jobs they claim since they do not actually go to work, or nearby business owners notice that no customers enter the fakers' business premises or that the fakers' lifestyle is much too lavish for someone who only works a few hours per week. The suspicion and negative impression is then applied to everything that person is and says.

Fortunately there are many positive aspects of BAM, one of which is that missionaries are often job makers. Job makers are those who see needs in the country and create businesses to meet the needs, improve the standards of living and employ nationals so that they may learn skills and earn a decent living. In the process they live out a Christian witness and share the gospel with their workers, clients and business network associates in appropriate levels of openness.

In the beginning years of the current wave of creative-access platforms and the subsequent burgeoning BAM strategy, many models were rushed forward. Amid all the experimenting and placement of personnel, some BAM models were not thought through in advance and have now been set aside. Many hard lessons were learned, but it was necessary to go down that road to find something that worked. BAM was recognized as one of the best models for getting people in, and in the beginning days some utilized landing pads that were not squeaky clean. With the experience gained and lessons learned, missionaries should anticipate and prepare for the future, avoiding the pitfalls of venturing into Christian ministry with dishonest platforms.

Needs Now and Needs to Come

In this book we are considering the interface of changes in the world with the unchanging mission that Christ gave his church. We need great wisdom to know when to change and when not to. While sending traditional missionaries was the norm for centuries, that ship may be sailing and the missions world must consider what's next. Mission agencies must be willing to make changes from time to time in order to be viable and effective, especially in the future. Regarding this, Jack Welch, the hugely successful former CEO of General Electric, said, "If the rate of change on the outside exceeds the rate of change on the inside, the end is near."[6] BAM and all efforts at creative-access platforms are only going to increase in necessity and require more creativity in the future, so the way we address missions needs must change.

Must Western missionaries be the front-line missionaries? Perhaps our most creative access would be to go to countries that we can enter more easily, and disciple, train and equip believers there to go to countries that may be closed to US citizens but more accessible to them. The West still contributes massive numbers of missionaries and more money in comparison to other nations, but our most important contribution might be to prepare and send God-called missionaries from the Global South. Yet, for them as well as for us, the need of the moment is to consider the needs of the future. What are the needs of the future that require specialized preparation and education for Christian workers so they can both meet needs and also be welcome in nations that will be closed or hostile to missionaries?

Most of the missionaries serving today are from churches in non-Western nations. Thousands of believers in the Latin American church are called to missions and long to have training in world religions, worldviews, intercultural communication and missiology, which will prepare them to serve effectively where God is calling them. Owing to the almost eight hundred years of sharing the Iberian Peninsula with Muslims from North Africa, Latin Americans share much in common with Muslim cultures, which facilitates their cultural adaptation. Chinese believers are also stepping out in missions service, especially in the "Back to Jerusalem" efforts, but as already noted they have a great need for missiological training and logistical support for that movement.[7] Is it too demeaning for Westerners to consider the possibility that a season of history has arrived when God wants us to serve in the role of preparation and sending rather than being those who wear pith helmets, swing machetes and preach in every service?

Terrorism is changing the way the world travels, communicates, does business and conducts daily life. While terrorism is as old as the ancient Assyrians invading and terrorizing the tribes of northern Israel, or pirates attacking sailing ships in early Protestant missions history, it is surging in frequency, ubiquity and technological prowess. Rather than reactively ministering to the suffering in the wake of terrorist attacks, missionaries should be proactive in ministry. This should also be the case regarding regional wars and rising crime in countries where missionaries live and serve. As mentioned earlier, governments and international businesses try to anticipate and meet oncoming world developments rather than react to crises after they have occurred. Such proactivity requires investment in forward thinking, studying recent and developing trends, and projecting possible solutions before the crisis ever happens. A perusal of financial or business magazines and websites reveals this kind of thinking. Businesses do not want to be caught flatfooted and be forced to chase their competition who was prepared for the changes. The stock market functions on the speculative purchases and investments made by people and firms who are trying to anticipate which stocks will drop or rise in value.

This chapter is not suggesting that a crystal ball or fortuneteller is necessary to devise missiological strategies or to prepare a BAM missionary force to meet the needs of the coming decades. Yet missionaries should not be outdone by the business world in an informed zeal to be ready for the days ahead. Forecasters are projecting stresses on the earth's resources and trends that missionaries should anticipate and incorporate into their plans.

THE COMING WORLD

The future missionary force must have the skills and training to meet the coming world. Medical science is rapidly developing medicines to immunize people against diseases and treat those that are inevitably struck in this fallen world. Pandemic threats from antibiotic resistant diseases, influenza or HIV will require skilled medical personnel in field missionary forces and administrations. The warming of global temperatures is enabling the migration of malaria-bearing mosquitoes to altitudes once considered safe, enabling malaria and other diseases to spread to new populations. Medical missionaries will always have a place in evangelical missions. BAM strategies must consider how the medical sector—those with skills and credentials for clinical and pharmaceutical research, and with educational expertise—could advance missions while meeting the needs of hurting people.

Developments in agriculture will provide food for the future that is more nutritious and plentiful. Educational systems and institutions throughout the world are improving their facilities and the quality of instruction. War-torn regions, areas devastated by natural disaster and economically challenged countries are looking beyond their own borders for help to rebuild and develop. Multinational business is more globalized today than at any other time. Research-and-development consulting firms, community-development businesses and nongovernmental organizations are increasingly needed and welcomed. It seems that the multiplying needs of the world are providing burgeoning opportunities for BAM models at the same time that countries are increasingly closing their doors to traditional missionaries. God makes all things beautiful in his time.

New Solutions

The scarcity of resources, which are being depleted at irresponsible levels, portend a global crisis. Certainly, if nothing changes, the coming crises will overwhelm plans to address them. Water shortages, famines, medical pandemics, politically belligerent factions bent on destroying all others and the dwindling oil reserves threaten to unravel the world.[8] Thus, we must make sure that we are preparing correctly in our BAM strategies and mission forces.

While some experts are forecasting depletion of oil reserves, the *Wall Street Journal* reports that much of the fear about the scarcity of the world's resources should be tempered with the knowledge that people have repeatedly broken through the barrier of limitations.[9] Rather than trusting in natural resources and hoping that more will be located, they emphasize that we should look to the innovation of new manmade or different natural resources. Matt Ridley cites experts who predicted that materials such as certain metals, petroleum or gas would run out, and then reports how populations either found alternatives, adjusted lifestyles or discovered that the predictions were not accurate.

Ernesto Sirolli related the findings of experts who were tasked in the 1860s with describing what New York City would be like one hundred years in the future. They studied the rapid growth rate of New York at that time and decided that the city would not exist one hundred years in the future. They reasoned that by then the city would require six million horses to transport the number of its residents and the amount of manure would be unmanageable, causing devastating disease.[10] Of course the problem is that they were basing all their calculations of the future on the world of their day. As we anticipate the future for missions and missionaries, we should remember that the world does not follow a linear path to the future.

One may wonder what the dynamics of geopolitics, diseases and the world's energy sources have to do with missions. The challenges facing the world's governments and gatekeepers are points where Christian workers should concentrate their preparation. It must be assumed that the world of the future will require more BAM and creative-access platforms, not fewer. In order to gain access to people who need the gospel, discipleship, churches, leadership training and holistic Christian ministry, missionaries must have the training and credentials that governments find desirable. In addition to simply gaining access, missionaries should have the skills, education, training and experience to be able to make a helpful difference in a hurting world.

Imagine hearing about a devastating disaster, such as a tsunami or an earthquake. Broken by the news footage depicting tens of thousands of homeless survivors, you immediately begin making plans to go to the disaster site to build new homes. Unfortunately you have no money, no knowledge of building materials or home design, and no construction experience. Such passion is zeal without knowledge. Likewise, hearing of injuries and subsequent diseases may move you to respond to relieve the suffering, but since you have no medical training, supplies or experience, you will be of little help in that situation. In fact, your zeal could cause more suffering than relief. It would be wiser to wait until you get the training or to help send those who do have training. But imagine that this natural disaster could have been predicted several years in advance, back when you were choosing your college major. Your life skills, career preparation and education credentials would have been developed to meet the need of the moment when the disaster came.

CONCLUSION

BAM is a strategy that not only enables Christian workers to enter and interact more openly in countries that are closed to traditional missionaries, it provides financial resources for living on the field since an international career position often pays very well. BAM also provides a natural network of relationships that develop through daily life and work. BAM is a way to open doors, obtain visas and earn a living, but more than anything it is a powerful strategy for reaching and teaching unreached and undiscipled people groups around the world.

The greatest impact of BAM may not necessarily be through young people with a missionary call but the host of retired Christian businessmen and women who can use their skills, resources, decades of experience and problem-solving wisdom to build relationships, meet people's needs and share the gospel in very natural settings. In the same way that a former US president serves as chairman of a global relief task force, or a veteran movie actor serves as an executive producer, retired businessmen and women bring their skills and life experience to the world missions table. Using BAM strategies will advance the cause of missions. When missionary candidates obtain MBAs or degrees in community development to get a visa, the years of preparation will be well spent. Christians living as Christians wherever God calls them provide a powerful testimony. However, BAM missions strategy and any creative-access platform should have integrity; there is no honor or wisdom in dishonesty. Pretending to be something you are not is damaging to the cause of Christ.

Young believers seeking a career in missions should examine today's trends that provide a glimpse into the future and ask how they could prepare to have the greatest impact. Anticipating and preparing to meet foreseeable needs through university majors and job experience will enable legitimate and needed ministry.

Empty nesters or retirees wanting to finish well should not be forced into a traditional missionary mold where they might not use the gifts, skills, experience and wisdom God has given them. Many middle-age people whose kids are grown and out of the house want to use their skills and resources on the mission field. God could use them as traditional evangelists and church planters in open countries, but their career skills as accountants, medical personnel, managers, construction, agriculture or a host of other careers could also be the perfect match for service in a creative-access country. When I lead retreats and spiritual emphasis weeks for mission agencies and language schools overseas, I increasingly meet older missionaries who retired early with a desire to spend the rest of their lives for the Lord on the mission field.

Reject the false dichotomy of meeting felt needs versus real needs. Some would suggest that the *real* need people have of hearing the gospel is all that missionaries should address. What did Jesus do? Which voice will be heard the most? The one who preaches and leaves? Or the one who preaches, helps, feeds, heals and ministers in practical ways? Which voice best represents what Jesus would do? Bringing educational credentials, job experience and needed skills can transform an otherwise suspicious scenario into genuine welcome. Meeting needs, making jobs and ministering to hurting people paves the way for gospel ministry.

Changing Governments

W E GOT OUT WITH THE CLOTHES WE WERE WEARING," the missionary couple said regarding their escape from the unrest in Rwanda. "Eventually we got a few of our things that were sent out after us, but it did not amount to much." Another family shared with me that they moved countries three times in their first four months on the field in West Africa, each time due to unrest, and each time with only what they were wearing or carrying in their hands. Another missionary related the terror of her kidnapping and period of captivity by Colombian Marxist guerrillas, while others told how they transferred out of the country just ahead of a kidnapping.

The governments of the countries where missionaries live and serve influence their ministries profoundly. This chapter is not intended to be a textbook on world governments or global politics. (I am not a political scientist.) But missiologists concerned with advancing the kingdom of God among the kingdoms of the world must have a basic awareness of the implications of changing governments. As a missiologist and ethnographer, I know the value of researching the cultures of the peoples to effectively minister among them. In like manner, international missionaries living outside of their home countries must be students of the cultures and governments where they live.

In this chapter I want to spin the globe and note some dynamic political realities and burgeoning trends that I believe will help missionaries. Certainly, a leader, party or government faction at the bottom of the pile in the morning can be on the top in the afternoon. Change is the only constant in the political realities of this world. All governments have laws and regulations that can change suddenly through a coup d'état or slowly over decades. As popular opinions change through immigration, ideological shifts, industrial developments or economic hardships, laws tend to shift as well. Missionaries should always seek to be exemplary residents and live within the law in every way biblically permissible. But to do so, the missionary must be politically aware. Our spiritual enemy influences governments to make decisions that increase physical and spiritual needs of people while simultaneously hindering the work of the church to address them. This chapter identifies some realities, trends and challenges in today's world with a few suggestions for faithfully promoting the glory of God among the nations.

Latin America and the Caribbean

Thinking about Caribbean island countries usually evokes images of peaceful beaches and vacation spots rather than political instability. However, history reveals tumultuous periods when Caribbean island nations were not peaceful locations for Christian ministry. Cuba comes to mind. Strife has been on the island long before the time of Castro. The United States' plunge into the Spanish-American War focused on the sinking of the *USS Maine* in Havana harbor (1898), and for centuries prior to that incident pirates had long harassed shipping and transportation. In more recent decades, the Castro government's identification with communism and repression of free speech has hampered Christian ministry on the island. Even though the Lord has been stirring his church in Cuba, government regulations continue to limit expansion of open ministry.

Cuba serves as an example of a country where Americans once owned property, traveled with ease and spent their vacations, but the world changed and missionaries were no longer welcome. Missionaries and pastors had once openly evangelized, discipled believers, started churches and formed seminaries. In a flash the country was turned upside down and closed to friendly missionary relationships. Cuba may reopen to evangelical missionaries in coming years, and very quickly when it does so. When Eastern Europe opened up after the fall of communism, there was a massive influx of ill-advised missions activity, and the local church there was not prepared for the Western invasion. Cuba's church is much more vital and vibrant than Eastern Europe's was. Many are seeking theological education and pastoral preparation, thus suggesting a healthier adjustment when doors open. It is also hoped that Western missionaries learned the lessons of rushing in with a zeal that lacks knowledge, as many did in Eastern Europe, and will be better prepared for the opportunities offered in that beautiful island nation to our south.[1]

The 2010 earthquake in Haiti destroyed much of the country's infrastructure and claimed around 200,000 lives. Although the earthquake did not cause all of the country's woes, it certainly brought them to the world's attention. In the process of seeking a solution to the devastation and bringing relief to the people, the world was forced to grapple with its pervasive poverty and political instability. Haiti continues to struggle with crippling poverty, massive amounts of rubble and the rebuilding of a country that was in great need long before the quake hit. The country's challenges, such as dependence on charcoal for fuel, have resulted in a barren land that is visibly different from its island-sharing neighbor, the Dominican Republic. "By some estimates, Haiti has lost 98 percent of its forests. Viewed from space, the island of Hispaniola is visibly brown and denuded on the Haitian, western side, while much of the Dominican Republic on the eastern side remains green. If ever the world needed stark evidence of the ravages of man-made desertification, Haiti is it."[2]

Like Cuba, Haiti was a Caribbean island nation where missionaries and mission teams once served without difficulty. However, a natural disaster rather than a coup d'état brought sudden changes in Haiti. The problems and questions in Haiti are many and complex; the answers must be as well. In a country whose religion is characterized by voodoo and syncretism, the spiritual needs are as vast as the physical ones. The people's trust in a stable government will be difficult to restore. How will present and future government administrations in Haiti guide it through this crisis?

The governments of Latin America, like governments in all nations, have seen ups and downs, peace and turmoil as they have struggled to find their place in the modern world. In some countries the storied past of dictatorships, military takeovers and "disappeared" people are told and retold, but only in hushed tones among safe company. Most of the Latin American countries went through revolutions to gain independence from Spain, periods of dysfunctional leadership, guerilla movements and political corruption. At various times they have been friends or enemies of the United States. The political trend of Latin American governments in recent years has been toward leftist governments, in some cases with a marked distaste for US policies on almost everything. Some of this is in response to the decades when US businesses were taking the profits from oil fields, banana plantations and gold mines. These companies used the local population to extract these resources in exchange for poor wages and few benefits. Many Latin American political leaders are frustrated that right-wing leaders in their own countries were involved with Western big businesses that facilitated the abuses. They now intend to reverse the alliance and repair the damage.

The days when Latin America could be considered a collection of sleepy banana republics ripe for the picking are thankfully over. But, unfortunately, businesspeople in the West made many enemies in the process of making their fortunes. Now many Latin American leaders successfully campaign on platforms of anti-Western rhetoric and seek friendships with nations that distrust the United States and Western big business. Following Castro's example of befriending and benefitting from the Soviet Union, other Latin leaders today are befriending and benefitting from China and Iran.

Latin American leaders often point to El Norte as the source of all their ills, whether or not this is precisely accurate. Castro pretended for years that the United States was on the brink of another invasion and used this ruse to keep the Cuban people united in willing resistance, strangely enough, even among those who said they knew better. Hugo Chavez led Venezuela in much the same way by constantly warning of an imminent US attack or a new assassination plot. Like Cuba, but often for different reasons, in a few short decades Latin America has gone from being an open mission field for traditional missionaries to one that is more difficult in many places and virtually impossible in others. Chavez responded to the unfortunate remarks of a misguided US televangelist by kicking out of Venezuela a US-based mission agency that had a long history of sacrificial and effective service. The fact that Chavez did so with a stroke of a pen and with virtually no backlash should serve as a warning.

The separation of peoples and classes based on wealth distribution usually leads to growing resentment, and socialist and leftist political preferences are seen more often in societies where the wealthy elites are perceived to have ridden to power on the backs of the working class. Because of this, Latin America has seen a rise in Marxist movements. Some forms of Christianity in those areas emphasize liberation theology, teaching that God has a preferential option for the poor and defending those who steal from the rich to give to the poor. Marxist thinking influences many governments of Latin America. This ideology enjoys popular support in Latin America due to the vast gap between the haves and have-nots.

The chasm between the powerful, wealthy few and the poor was seen most notably during the Spanish conquest and the ensuing period of colonialism. The indigenous people were enslaved to serve the conquerors, until Spain outlawed indigenous slavery. Then they were virtually enslaved through the *reducción*, *encomienda* and *hacienda* systems. In the twentieth century, land reform acts were passed to redistribute the land, taking it from wealthy families and the Roman Catholic Church, and dividing it more fairly among the indigenous masses. This class-struggle mentality harmonizes well with ideals of Marxism and even blends into the theology of Latin America's liberation theology, which was promoted prolifically by Peruvian priest Gustavo Gutiérrez. A desire to empower the impoverished combines with distaste for the wealthy West in much of Latin America's politics and government regulations taking shape today. This results in significant changes in governmental policies, such as visa requirements and governmental recognition of churches, and mission challenges shaped by the negative perception of missionaries.

Although geographically Brazil could be considered part of Latin America, differences in language—Portuguese instead of Spanish—and its recent economic influence lead many to consider it separately. The country's massive size, roughly equivalent to the continental United States, and its diversity of ethnolinguistic people groups, religions and regions, set it apart. Brazil is home to the Amazon River, the world's largest river system of over eleven hundred tributaries, draining one-sixth of the world's fresh water into the ocean. The government protects the Amazon's uncontacted indigenous tribes from contact by outsiders, including evangelical missionaries.

Brazil is also home to some of the world's largest urban areas, São Paulo alone boasts around twenty million people and Rio de Janeiro counts over twelve million. Some of the world's largest cults—such as the Universal Church of the Kingdom of God—were birthed and are still headquartered in Brazil. This spiritually diverse region of the world has also witnessed massive growth and church planting among evangelicals, such as the rapidly multiplying Assemblies of God churches being planted in Belém. Brazil was counted among the economic powerhouse countries in the first decade of the second millennium, but that growth has begun to falter. As Brazil prepared for the 2014 World Games, many of its poorer and middle-class citizens protested that great expense, arguing the funds should have been used for hurting socioeconomic segments. Rioting and demonstrations of frustration with the government ensued.

The current president, Dilma Rousseff, was recently narrowly reelected in a fiercely contested runoff election, and her administration is facing a struggling economy, as are many of her Latin American neighbors. The Brookings Institute notes, "By the end of 2014, 12 Latin American countries will have had presidential elections over the past two years. After a decade of strong growth, the region faces a troubling combination of decelerating economies and rising social expectations." It asks, "How will governments respond and what are the implications for the direction of social, economic, trade, and foreign policy in Latin America?"[3] That is the question for mission agencies, missiologists and missionaries as well. We must anticipate these developments and be prepared for them as they unfold rather than react after the fact.

Asia

Central Asia includes the area of the "stans," republics that formerly belonged to the Soviet Union, specifically, Kazakhstan, Kyrgyzstan, Tajikistan, Turkmenistan and Uzbekistan. The governments here are considered republics, but the bulk of power and authority to rule rests with the president of each. The religion in this part of the world is predominantly Islam, though there is a prior history of Hinduism, Buddhism, Nestorian Christianity, Judaism and Zoroastrianism. Missionaries in this part of the world enter on visas with skills that will be helpful to the local population and facilitate a creative-access platform for ministry. Since the breakup of the Soviet Union, Russia desires the restoration of closer relations with these nations. Missionaries in this area of the world should remain vigilant for political developments and negative attitudes toward Westerners.

South Asia includes the countries of Afghanistan, Bangladesh, Bhutan, India, Maldives, Nepal, Pakistan and Sri Lanka. The list of these countries' religions includes almost all of the world's major religions, although almost two-thirds of the people are Hindus, and almost one-third are Muslims. The largest country in this region is India, which rivals China as the most populous country in the world. While there is no legal enforcement of caste, and indeed laws exist to prohibit discrimination against the lowest castes, many still live according to caste rules and social division. India has been rising in recent years due to its burgeoning influence as South Asia's "Silicon Valley" and the hub of big business. However, its meteoric rise is slowing. *Business Insider* reports that India, along with the other BRICS countries of Brazil, Russia, China and South Africa, is on the way down economically. (The economies of the MINT countries—Mexico, Indonesia, Nigeria and Turkey—are surging.)[4]

Known as the largest communist country today, China moved from being the Qing Dynasty to the Republic of China in 1912, and then to the People's Republic of China in 1949. Missionaries have found China's doors open or closed to greater or lesser degrees through many years. What seems unchanging about China today is its embrace of communism, including human rights abuses and persecution of Christians.

Even so, the church continues to grow in numbers and boldness in communist China. Some forecast that China will be the world's most Christian nation by 2030.[5] And the coastal city of Wenzhou has been called China's Jerusalem. Home to an estimated two thousand churches, Wenzhou has suffered the demolition of church buildings and the removal of more than three hundred crosses on other church buildings in a crackdown on Christianity that began in the mid-2010s. Some believers with painful memories of government-sponsored attacks fear a renewed persecution of Christians.

China's influence on countries nearby and around the world is substantial. China not only supports and protects the communist countries of Asia, it is active in business, making massive government loans to countries as far away as Latin America. An audacious plan to dig a new canal across Central America through Nicaragua has been launched by a Chinese billionaire businessman Wang Jing.[6] The 130-mile Interoceanic Grand Canal is estimated to require around $50 billion, of which Jing will contribute about $300 million of his own. The ultimate success of the project depends on the Chinese government.[7] Burgeoning Chinese influences throughout the Americas, Africa, Asia and Europe are clearly visible. Howard French's book *China's Second Continent: How a Million Migrants Are Building a New Empire in Africa* details the influence China is having in that massive continent.[8] *Forbes* reports, "China should not be seen as 'one of the BRICS' or as 'another emerging economy.' China is the emerging global great power, the first in over a century, following the United States' great power emergence dating back to the 1898/99 Spanish-American War."[9]

The countries of Southeast Asia are also having more influence in world business and politics. With Indonesia's economy surging, the region will have more say and play on the world stage. Indonesia is home to more Muslims than any other nation, and other Southeastern Asian nations, such as Malaysia and the Philippines, are also home to many Muslims.

Islam's pervasive influence has been likened to a three-stranded rope. One strand represents the cultural rules of life, another is the legal system and the third is the religious practices. Looking at an individual strand on the end of the rope and trying to recognize which is the same strand fifty feet down the rope's length is impossible. Similarly, trying to discern why a person acted as he or she did in such cultures is analogous to asking which strand caused them to do so. When wound tightly together, the strands become one, just as all aspects of life in Muslim cultures blend together. Missionaries must be aware of the trend toward more conservative and fundamentalist forms of Islam, even in the countries of Southeast Asia, and concentrate on those areas where there is still an open door for ministry. With a growing economic base, these countries will not require the cooperation and assistance of the "Christian" West and will be afforded the luxury of choosing friends and making policies that may be more gospel hostile in the future.

SUB-SAHARAN AFRICA

Sub-Saharan Africa nations have seen Islam moving southward into their areas through legal political means as well as through violence, as is seen in Nigeria's Boko Haram, Kenya's Al-Shabaab and the strife in Sudan. Terrifying headlines related to Boko Haram report how the group has murdered students in Western-style schools and has kidnapped hundreds of young girls in its wave of terror. BBC reports,

Nigeria's militant Islamist group Boko Haram—which has caused havoc in Africa's most populous country through a wave of bombings, assassinations and abductions—is fighting to overthrow the government and create an Islamic state. Its followers are said to be influenced by the Koranic phrase which says: "Anyone who is not governed by what Allah has revealed is among the transgressors." Boko Haram promotes a version of Islam which makes it "haram," or forbidden, for Muslims to take part in any political or social activity associated with Western society. This includes voting in elections, wearing shirts and trousers or receiving a secular education.[10]

This violence against anything Western and non-Muslim is focused on Christians, and entire villages have been murdered in recent years. The instability of government political systems and divisive rivalries in some African countries render their presidents and armies virtually paralyzed against such violence.

Although the peoples of Africa have rich cultures with long histories of vast empires and storied reigns of powerful leaders, most of Africa was eventually colonized by Western nations until the 1950s, when countries began to gain their independence. Between 1950 and 1980 almost all of the African countries became independent, with their own democratic political rule. However, in many African countries, tribal divisions have resulted in a virtual gang-rule state, whose leaders are untouchable power bosses. The poverty in some countries has fomented networks of fraud, theft and even piracy on the high seas. The tragic superstitious notion that raping a virgin will cure a man of AIDS has resulted in assaults on many young girls and the consequent spread of this disease, which is still a death sentence for the poor. In addition to this plague, malaria frequently kills in Africa. The pandemic of Ebola in West Africa continues to expand its deadly grip. Some see these struggles with broken political systems, disease and religious syncretism as an unassailable combination of evils. The violent spread of Islam, political instability and incurable diseases in sub-Saharan Africa are forces for missionaries to watch with daily vigilance. It would be inaccurate to say that these are "trends" in Africa, as if they are new developments. Rather, they are simply the continuation of problems that have been developing over decades. If there is anything new, it is the acceleration of these problems.

NORTH AFRICA AND THE MIDDLE EAST

North Africa and the Middle East consist of countries that have seen violent political turnover in recent years through uprisings and coups in what has been dubbed the Arab Spring. The *Oxford Dictionary* defines Arab Spring as "a series of antigovernment uprisings in various countries in North Africa and the Middle East, beginning in Tunisia in December 2010."[11] While manifestations have included riots, protests, revolutions and coups, which have occurred for a variety of reasons, a common root of the rebellion has been a desire to be free from tyrannical dictators. Unfortunately, replacement governments have struggled to govern rival factions, and thus social and political volatility continues.

Some countries have made it illegal for their citizens to change their religion and for missionaries to evangelize. They also allow for discrimination against Christians. However, the fact that a country's majority population is Muslim does not necessarily mean that all Christian activity is illegal, is in hiding and is disappearing. I have preached and taught legally in countries of the Arab Peninsula, and was treated very kindly by all while I was there. Indeed, some Christian ministers in the United Arab Emirates are there on religious worker visas to serve the churches that are legally recognized. Unfortunately, as is widely documented and increasingly the case, most of the other countries in the region are far more restrictive and oppressive.

No mention of governments in this region can omit reference to the recent phenomenon of ISIS. A murderous threat against Christianity is growing in North Africa and the Middle East. A terrorist movement called ISIS, claiming to be a new state in search of a territory, is growing in strength with unprecedented extremes of violence throughout the region. "The Islamic State of Iraq and the Levant (Isis) has taken over from the al-Qa'ida organisation founded by Osama bin Laden as the most powerful and effective extreme jihadi group in the world. . . . The last 's' of 'Isis' comes from the Arabic word 'al-Sham,' meaning Levant, Syria or occasionally Damascus, depending on the circumstances."[12]

In addition to public beheadings, crucifixions and shootings of Christians, the rapidly advancing group regularly uses social and news media to broadcast the execution of Christians and even other Muslims they consider to be enemies. They use video to heighten the effects of terror, usually for high-profile killings such as the decapitation of known Western reporters and aid workers or for more horrific carnage—multiple beheadings on a beach or burning to death a caged Jordanian pilot after soaking him in gasoline.

The burgeoning number of groups that have sworn allegiance to or identified with ISIS include the Boko Haram in Nigeria, Al Shabaab in Kenya and similar groups in Algeria, Pakistan, Afghanistan, Gaza, Lebanon, Yemen, Egypt, Libya, India, Chechnya, Philippines and China.[13] Reports have circulated that ISIS envisions a five-year plan to control North Africa, portions of southern Europe, the Middle East and Central Asia as their state territory. While other reports quickly surfaced branding this plan as a fake or fantasy, the developing trend of ISIS is that a five-year plan with such limited scope might be too conservative. After the April 2015 martyrdom of thirty Ethiopian Christians by bullets and beheadings, an ISIS spokesman declared to the world, "We swear to Allah: the one who disgraced you by our hands, you will not have safety, even in your dreams, until you embrace Islam."[14] Whether ISIS will become a new state with which legitimate world governments will carry out diplomacy and trade is yet to be seen, but unfortunately not out of the question.

EUROPE

Politically, the governments of Western Europe tend to be social democracies. Religiously, Christianity came to the Americas from Western Europe. Now Christianity in Western Europe has become both secularized and marginalized, while other religions have grown stronger. Islam arrived in Western Europe centuries ago through invasion and traveling merchants. It continues arriving daily from West Africa, North Africa and the Middle East. Both Muslim and Hindu immigrants arrive as refugees from political strife and economic woes, or for business opportunities and education. This influx of immigrants has influenced the local cultural contexts and worldviews as well. The burden to care for the burgeoning number of poorer immigrants has contributed to economic hardships and instability for European governments.

An in-depth comparative analysis of the politics of Western Europe is of course beyond our scope here, but a glance at the history of Western civilization reveals that this region of the world is rich in political upheaval. It has played host to two world wars and the rise and fall of many leaders who were both politically and religiously motivated. From the sacking of Rome to confronting the Muslim invasion, to the Reformation, to today's effects of globalization, Western Europe has been and will continue to be one of the most important regions in the world. In some countries evangelical Christians number less than 2 percent of the population. Assuming that Western Europe has been reached by the gospel and that it favors evangelical Christianity is a grave mistake. Western Europe must return to a place of prominence in our missions priorities. It remains an influential power broker in world politics, but is now steeped in secular post-Christian worldviews. Europe must be reevangelized.

Eastern Europe is a postcommunist region in the throes of strife and reconfiguration even as this chapter is being written. After the fall of the Iron Curtain and the breakup of the Soviet empire, nations formerly belonging to the Soviet Union regained their independence. During the mid-2010s, Russian president Vladimir Putin signaled his desire to regain former Soviet satellite republics. In early 2014 Russia assisted a rebellion against the pro-European Union western region of Ukraine by enabling and supporting the pro-Russian dissidents in Crimea and the eastern side of Ukraine. Since this unrest continues, some missionaries have been evacuated and others remain on high alert and wary of unrest. Former Eastern Bloc nations' economies are dependent on Russian natural gas and oil to greater or lesser degrees. Politicians are sometimes easily persuaded to side with whoever offers the most financial aid and benefit. Recent events in Ukraine serve as an example of how governments that seem stable and friendly to Westerners can become unstable, volatile and even explosively violent overnight.

NORTH AMERICA

Mexico, Canada and the United States are experiencing political and governmental changes driven by immigration and the resulting cultural changes. They, like parts of Western Europe, are witnessing the growing pains of burgeoning Muslim immigrant populations that insist on recognition of lifestyles and even legal regulations in harmony with sharia law.

School systems are faced with the diversity of immigrants' languages. Courts must provide interpreters for speakers of these languages, and government resettlement of refugees includes providing them ESL and job skills. To what degree will the laws of the United States change to extend protection of all rights? And when such laws are passed and enforced, how will that affect evangelical ministers and ministries in North America?

The changes we are experiencing in North America, and the way these changes potentially shape our laws, reveal the ways our governments might change. These changes result in vastly different ministry contexts as well as shifting legal frameworks within which ministry must be done.

IDEOLOGIES OF INFLUENCE

Now, let's look at some key ideologies behind these realities. Those we minister to have a worldview shaped in part by their government, and therefore when we minister interculturally we must be aware of global governmental ideologies.

Sharia law. Among the countries that practice sharia law, the enforcement of those laws and the penalties for breaking them is not uniform. In some countries the penalty for either converting to Christianity or committing adultery is the same: death. Technically, the word *sharia* means "the path to a watering hole," which implies it is simply an ethical way of living rather than a compilation of legal codes.[15] This system, derived from the teachings of the Koran and the life of Muhammad, is applied and enforced in national judicial systems to greater or lesser degrees in over fifty countries that are members of the Organisation of Islamic Conference.[16] Some offenses against sharia law are specifically dealt with and carry particular punishments. *Guardian* writer Susie Steiner reported on the Nigerian death sentence handed down to a woman accused of adultery, explaining that the severe penalty was due to the crime being classified as a "Hadd offense."

> Hadd offences carry specific penalties, set by the Koran and by the prophet Mohammed. These include unlawful sexual intercourse (outside marriage); false accusation of unlawful intercourse; the drinking of alcohol; theft; and highway

robbery. Sexual offences carry a penalty of stoning to death or flogging while theft is punished with cutting off a hand.[17]

The sentence for converting from Islam to another religion may be death even though the Koran does not demand death for apostasy from Islam. Death of the apostate is sometimes sought through legal charges in the courts or more informally through brutal "honor killings." When legal procedures are used to seek execution, it is normally under the umbrella of a charge of treason. The Council on Foreign Relations' website states,

> How does sharia law view religious conversion?
>
> Conversion by Muslims to other faiths is forbidden under most interpretations of sharia and converts are considered apostates (non-Muslims, however, are allowed to convert into Islam). Some Muslim clerics equate this apostasy to treason, a crime punishable by death. The legal precedent stretches back to the seventh century when Prophet Mohammed ordered a Muslim man to death who joined the enemies of Islam at a time of war.[18]

Certainly, evangelism and open conversion would be strictly forbidden in stricter sharia law enforcement contexts, so missionaries must be aware of both the cultural mores and the laws of the countries they live in. Moreover, it is essential to be aware of all changes that are occurring in this influential and highly volatile part of the world.

As changes develop in one region, other countries that previously practiced sharia law informally have begun to pass legislation making it the law of the land. Some have dubbed this as the official "Islamification" of their countries. In 2013, Libya voted to make sharia law the law of the land. Al Jazeera reported,

> Libya's National Assembly has voted to make Sharia, Islamic law, the foundation of all legislation and state institutions in

the country. The immediate scope of the General National Congress's (GNC) decision on Wednesday was not clear, but a special committee will review all existing laws to guarantee they comply with Islamic law. "Islamic law is the source of legislation in Libya," the GNC said in a statement after the vote. "All state institutions need to comply with this."[19]

More recently, Brunei voted to join the list of nations that have adopted sharia law as binding. Brunei is the first country in Asia to officially do so, although provinces in Malaysia and Indonesia had previously voted to adopt sharia law as their official legal system.[20] Whether Brunei becomes the first domino to fall in a trend of new legal system adoptions or not, there are already a number of countries with varying degrees of enforcement. *The Huffington Post* reported in 2013,

> In countries with classical Shariah systems, Shariah has official status or a high degree of influence on the legal system, and covers family law, criminal law, and in some places, personal beliefs, including penalties for apostasy, blasphemy, and not praying. These countries include Egypt, Mauritania, Sudan, Afghanistan, Iran, Iraq, the Maldives, Pakistan, Qatar, Saudi Arabia, Yemen, and certain regions in Indonesia, Malaysia, Nigeria, and the United Arab Emirates. Mixed systems are the most common in Muslim-majority countries. Generally speaking, Shariah covers family law, while secular courts will cover everything else. Countries include: Algeria, Comoros, Djibouti, Gambia, Libya, Morocco, Somalia, Bahrain, Bangladesh, Brunei, Gaza Strip, Jordan, Kuwait, Lebanon, Malaysia, Oman, and Syria.[21]

Of course, Libya and Brunei have now moved from the second of these lists into the first.

Communism, socialism and leftist politics. Communism is a sociopolitical system that claims the collective ownership of everything and promotes a classless society, which so far only works on paper. Communist countries have been historically brutal in their repression of Christian activity, especially during the Cold War. Since the fall of the Iron Curtain, China, North Korea, Laos, Vietnam and Cuba continue the tradition, with North Korea leading the gang in ruthless persecution of Christians.[22] Leftist political views are closely related to ideals of communism. The primary goal in the rhetoric is the liberation of the poor and oppressed masses.

Leftist politicians have found favor in the eyes of many in Latin America since the liberation of Cuba by the hands of Fidel Castro, Che Guevara and their band of "freedom fighters." Che soon left Cuba hoping to replicate their victory in Congo and Bolivia. He was unsuccessful in both and was killed in Bolivia, allegedly by the bullets of CIA operatives. Leftist guerilla movements throughout Latin America have sought to free their countries from ruling parties tied to corruption, big business and Western powers. It is no surprise that leftist leaders also tend to be socialistic in their politics. Socialism embraces the notion that major industries should be entrusted to the people, that is, the state. For this reason it is common to see leftist leaders in Latin America nationalizing natural gas, petroleum, mining and so forth, because these resources belong to the people and therefore so should the proceeds and profits, not to the big companies that extract them.

While Latin America's leftist governments influenced by socialism or communism do not necessarily impede or restrict evangelical Christianity, such governments' desire to weed out cults may sweep along evangelical missionaries in restrictive legislation. For instance, requiring that all legal church activities be conducted in buildings with ministers who have been duly ordained or certified by a recognized denomination in the country may simply be an effort to root out the newly arriving cults. Unfortunately, evangelical churches that begin with home prayer groups and Bible studies are lumped into the same category. In addition, many evangelical missionaries from the United States are unfairly identified as representatives of US politics and foreign policies. This, coupled with the stain of paternalistic missions methods during the last half of the twentieth century, often creates negative impressions.

Missionary Life in Challenging Political Environments

Mission agencies read news reports from around the world and subscribe to international news bulletins as a matter of necessity. Missionaries should find solid sources of news that accurately report on current events in the places they serve. Rigidly open or closed countries do not exist; rather countries are somewhere on the continuum and moving in one direction or another. A coup, an election, a leader's death or a natural disaster can drastically change the openness of a country to Western missionaries, specifically from the United States. Even in the absence of those major events, the actions of a few missionaries lacking in discernment can endanger all the Christian workers in a country.

The world's governments are not inept, and their intelligence gathering capabilities are often quite sophisticated. Yet it does not require highly trained officers to know that something is afoot when you are the only one in your neighborhood who encrypts emails. Government intelligence agencies have broken enough codes to figure out what you mean when you email people in your home country to report that you gave out "manuals" to new "members" of your "club" at the "swim meet" you held last Sunday night as you "yarped giving thanks to Dad." I do not mean to belittle those who must find some terms for communication that are not easily Googled or recognized by Web crawlers; this is certainly a legitimate challenge. I simply want to emphasize that governments usually know of your presence. If you have a maid, everyone she knows also knows what happens in your home. If you have children, the neighbors' children, and therefore the neighbors, usually know what is going on in your family.

I was visiting a Christian worker in Asia, who held the highest security level in his organization for a creative-access country, when his mail arrived. It came to the mailbox at his home, clearly labeled from his sending agency and directed to Reverend _____. As we later went to a new restaurant in a neighboring town, the waiter greeted him as "pastor" as he took our order. Since such stories are true and commonplace, why aren't more missionaries arrested or expelled? In most countries, the government is not so concerned about missionaries' presence unless they are making waves. If they maintain a low profile in their work and remain under the radar as much as possible, they should be able to continue. When missionaries cause an incident or their activities create public awareness and concern, they force the government's hand and the authorities must act. Most governments maintain the attitude of "just do not embarrass us." Do them that favor.

Governments and national politics can change with dizzying velocity. Be careful about identifying too closely with the political leaders and power brokers of the day. When entering new communities in more accessible environments that accept evangelistic activity, church planting and Christian presence, we should always introduce ourselves to the authorities and let them know why we are there and what we are doing. An old adage holds, "Whatever people aren't up on, they are usually down on." When an Andean community mayor learns of a team of foreigners going door-to-door in his town talking with his people, it is his job to become suspicious. However, taking a few minutes to stop by his office for coffee and simple introductions has gained missionaries wide open doors and assurances of safety. Even so, respectful interaction does not require revealing everything we know or ingratiating ourselves to develop a close relationship. Becoming too closely identified with a president, governor or mayor of a particular political party or faction can be unwise in places where politics shift with the wind.

A good practice is to avoid politics completely in conversations. When a conversation discusses some character flaw in the president of our own country, we should not join the conversation. Many group-oriented cultures will not respect someone who speaks ill of their own leaders. If they are belittling their own leaders, pointing out some corrupt practice coming to light in the local news, do not join in. When I was growing up, I could fight with my sister, but no one else could!

Because we are from North America, people will inevitably bring up US politics or foreign policies. They will rarely understand these topics well enough to discuss or critique wisely, but they will do so anyway. It requires great patience to remain silent and allow them their say. A safe reply is to remind them that we do not represent our government and so cannot speak to its policies. Remember that we are ambassadors of the King, not of the president.

Finally, remember the open door that missionaries once had and took for granted in places like Venezuela, Russia, China and Cuba. The last three countries in this list may seem out of place in such a statement, but the truth is that in certain periods of history, missionaries served Christ in those countries and thought that someone would always do so. Remember that doors that open can also close; missionary visas granted today may be denied tomorrow. When we have an open door for ministry, we must be active in evangelizing evangelists, discipling disciplers and teaching teachers so the work will continue with or without our presence.

Missionaries must pay attention to their host government so they are aware of any changes occurring and are vigilant about implications for their ministries. They must also have an informed perspective so they can address ethical implications. Missionaries must submit to the laws, norms and regulations of countries whenever possible. I say "whenever possible" because the laws of the King outweigh and overrule the laws of kings. When the laws of the land forbid or command anything counter to what the Lord has clearly commanded or forbidden in his Word, our way is clear. Obedience to God should characterize our lives, and in most cases we can obey in ways that both honor him and attract others to Christ.

When moving to a different country, on arrival international missionaries should register with their government's embassy so that the embassy can contact or assist them in case of emergency. US embassies and consulates around the world maintain contact with registered citizens through Warden System emails with information relevant to US citizens.[23] We should not place our security in naive ignorance. There is nothing spiritual about being blissfully unaware. Just as we would take precautions during hurricane season in Florida, we must be aware of the ever-developing political climate in our host country and have an action plan in place.

Paul tells us in Romans 13 to be subject to the governing authorities because God has instituted them. As frustrating as government red tape can be, and as demoralizing as bureaucracy often is, God has sent or allowed every king, president and prime minister. Moreover, Paul tells us to pray for kings and all those in authority so that we may lead a peaceful and quiet life (1 Timothy 2:1-2). Missionaries cannot predict every political wind that may blow in coming years, but we may concentrate on being good citizens of Christ's kingdom while living in and ministering to citizens in other kingdoms. Remember that gospel-hostile governments and their rulers are not our enemies; they are prisoners of war. The enemy has blinded them to do his will. He is relentless in his attacks; we must be relentless in our advance. The gates of hell will not prevail against us.

The Global South, Southern Church and Role of Western Missionaries

THERE HAS NOT ONLY BEEN a population shift to the Global South but a power shift as well. The term *Global South* has nothing to do with the Mason-Dixon line; it refers primarily to the nations that lie south of the equator and that have been historically referred to as developing nations, the Third World, the Two-Thirds World or the Majority World. Todd Johnson of the World Christian Database has explored trends for the growth of Christianity in the coming years. One key trend is that Christianity continues to move south and east. What was once considered a Western religion is increasingly less so. This shift results in three key implications for the church. Our understanding of Christianity has been defined by the Western church's theological contributions, but as the church in the south and east grows, so will its influence in shaping our understanding of theology and the world's understanding of what it means to be Christian. A second implication of the growth of Christianity in the south and east is a change in the dominant language(s) of the faith. A third key implication of this geographic shift is that large pockets of Christians will live in near-neighbor cultures and close proximity to Muslims, Hindus and Buddhists. Missionaries must prayerfully consider the missiological implications and what this might mean for ministry endeavors.[1]

The Global South has an increasingly significant role on the world stage even though many areas still tend to be characterized by destabilization and corruption. However, this part of the world is also responsive to Christianity. Sadly, the crippling strain of poverty and oppression has led many to grasp after straws held out by extreme forms of health-and-wealth heresies and liberation theology. Additionally, there has been a sweeping Pentecostalization of this area of the world. How should evangelical Christian missionaries interpret and interact with the legalism and emphasis on the miraculous gifts, signs and wonders often found in these churches? This chapter will address some realities of the Global South and its church, and consider the future role of Western missionaries. The growth of the southern church is surprising to some who think of these areas as the unreached parts of the world, so we must first consider the whos, wheres and whys of where we go to do what we do.

REACHING THE UNREACHED

Who are the unreached? The unreached people groups are not all in Central, South, East or Southeast Asia; they are found in every part of the world. Consider the Americas, which are often perceived to be "reached." Of the 999 people groups in the Americas, over two-thirds of them are unreached when employing the "2 percent or more evangelical" criterion that is the generally utilized missiological guideline. Over one-third of people groups in North, Central and South America are not only unreached, they are unengaged, which means that in the last two years no one has been trying to engage them with a church-planting movement. Additionally, almost 10 percent of them are "uncontacted," having never been contacted by someone from outside their group for the purpose of evangelism.[2] When I've shared these statistics with individuals in the past, they've often remarked that they had no idea there were unreached peoples in the Americas, much less so many. This is just one example of how terms can often be misunderstood, leading to well-intentioned misapplication. It is helpful to know what terms mean when speaking of the unreached, and what others understand by the same terms.

Significant confusion surrounds the term *unreached*, making it one of the most misleading descriptors in missions today.[3] *Unreached* means that there is not a biblically responsible indigenous church strong enough to continue the work among them without outside help. It does not mean that no one among them has heard the gospel; nor does it refer to an arbitrary percentage, whether 2 percent or 80 percent, below which a culture is unreached and once that threshold is crossed they are reached and therefore need no more effort from outsiders. Even the missiologists who coined the term did not intend such an application.

To understand the implications of the misuse of the term, consider what the opposite term *reached* would mean by implication. Does *reached* mean that a group has heard the gospel one time, as in a weeklong evangelistic campaign? Does it mean that a certain number of people raised their hands to "accept Christ"? How many times did you "hear" the gospel before you heard the gospel? When looking at levels of being reached, we must consider whether the gospel was presented to a people group in a culturally appropriate way and clearly preached in the local language so they could rightly understand the gospel and its implications for their lives. Or would *reached* mean that a people group heard the gospel and truly believed it, even though no one among them has been discipled or trained to interpret and apply the Scriptures? If so, what will

become of the rest of the people group and subsequent generations? Considering a group to be reached is challenging since virtually every group is unreached by someone's interpretation. What
is the bare minimum that constitutes a reached people group such
that we should not expect the Holy Spirit to call any missionaries
to serve?

Rightly understanding the term *unreached* greatly facilitates
the work facing missionaries in the twenty-first century and beyond.
When groups that have clustered themselves linguistically, racially,
ethnically and culturally have no New Testament church or discipled Christians to evangelize them, they effectively constitute an
unreached group or an unreached segment of a group. Missiologists debate whether an immigrant group should be considered
unreached if in their home countries a tribe that goes by the same
name is more than 2 percent Christian. The gospel culture in the
home country is hardly beneficial for those who are cut off from
there. Moreover, these immigrant groups are often marginalized
from the dominant cultures of their host countries as well. Displaced persons, whether from persecution, disaster or economic
immigration in this day of globalization and urbanization, may constitute unreached segments of peoples who we must learn to recognize and engage.

Where are the unreached? Unreached people groups, and
segments of them, are increasingly found in the most unlikely
places. While we might expect to find them in the Amazon's jungles,
Asia's islands and Africa's arid regions, they are increasingly found
in the capital cities and urban sprawls of the Global South. In some
of the countries where I travel, one-third to one-half of their populations live in the capital cities. The United Nations reports that
over half of the world's population lives in urban areas.[4] The trend
is not slowing; by 2050 an additional 2.5 billion are predicted to live
in urban areas.[5] Yet, just because numerous people groups are

teeming in megacities, it does not mean that they are all alike. Urban missionaries must keep in mind that as people move to the cities of the Global South, they bring their cultures and worldviews with them.

Additionally, where the unreached are located today is not necessarily where they will be tomorrow. The world maps in contemporary missions books are often tinted with colors according to religious preference or dominance of each region. Students often mistakenly believe that the Muslim, Buddhist or Hindu-colored areas of the world are monolithic bastions of those religions, and regions where Christianity has never taken root. It would be interesting to study the world's regions in a diachronic fashion, tracking the rise and fall of different religions through the centuries. Some of today's most resistant gospel-hostile areas were once Christian regions with strong Christian influence and even home to great churches and seminaries. A diachronic glance over the last century of Europe would provide us a modern-day illustration of this dynamic process of religion shifting around the world. Regions that were once strongly Christian, training theologians and sending missionaries, have given way to secularism and the religious imperialism of invading forces.

Should the Lord tarry, the day will come when believers in the southern church notice that Europe is an unreached continent and turn their eyes northward to reach and teach Europe.[6] When that day comes, will anyone remember that Europe was once heavily Christian and the cradle of evangelical Christianity? The southern church will then plant churches and contextualize the kind of Christianity in Europe that they know and practice in their home countries. It is crucial to ensure that they are thoroughly biblical in their doctrine and practice, both because the southern church is assuming such a pivotal role in the global Christian drama and because Christ has commanded us to do so. The future reevangelization that they will bring to Europe will then have to be repeated in the United States as well. The churches of the Global South will likely reengage and reevangelize North America. If what passes for evangelical Christianity in much of the Global South today were to be replicated in the United States, would we recognize our churches? Would they be more or less biblical? Would they be healthier or weaker reflections of New Testament teaching? The answers to those questions are more or less encouraging as we consider the myriad manifestations of churches around the world. But in the places where we simply evangelized and moved on without discipling and teaching, the forms of Christianity tend to be blended with traditional religions and definitely are not conducive to the future of a healthy evangelical Christianity.

Why are they unreached? It is true that there are places and peoples in the world where the gospel is not known. It is also true that some places and people have had gospel proclamation in the recent or distant past but without discipleship of the believers, training of leadership and preparation for ongoing healthy Christian ministry. What is often seen in those places is barely recognizable through New Testament eyes.

Notwithstanding all of the emphasis on unreached people groups today, the reality of most missionaries will not be serving in a place where no one has ever heard of Christianity. Over half of the world's people groups may truly be less than 2 percent evangelical, but there are relatively few entire people groups in the world where everyone in the group is 100 percent ignorant of the gospel. But wherever they are we must reach them with the gospel at any cost. Still, the greater need today and for decades to come will be to reenter those areas that were engaged to some degree in the past but were left too early to form a healthy church that is self-propagating, self-governing and self-supporting.

Leaving behind undiscipled and untaught peoples requires

other missionaries to return in the future and reevangelize people groups, disciple them and train leaders among them. This task is even harder for missionaries for two reasons. First, sending churches sometimes do not value such ministry as true missions work since they are not reaching the unreached. Second, these cultures often consider themselves Christian, even though syncretism or aberrant theology is prolific and profound. Missionaries must then decontextualize before they can truly recontextualize the gospel and Christianity in that place. The difficulty of decontextualization is that it seems the trusted teacher (the first missionary who loved the people and was loved by them) is being attacked by the dismantling of their original understanding of Christianity. Because of their loyalty to the pioneer missionary, new missionaries are seen as meddlers and are often rejected along with any suspicious "new" teaching.

When missionaries focus on reaching the unreached as the most crucial need of the hour, they often push to reach the unreached as quickly as possible. That sounds both logical and necessary. Preachers in missions conferences often call their hearers to reach the unreached, thinking that missionaries who accept the challenge will enter unreached groups, preach the gospel and stay to teach them all Christ commanded. The problem arises almost immediately after these missionaries obtain a beachhead. Since for them "missions equals reaching the unreached," they feel that they must leave the fledgling gathering of believers sooner rather than later and press on to the next place, or they are not really doing missions, which God has called them to do.

Certainly, there are some places in the world where the gospel is not known, and most of them are in the Global South. Yet there are many more places where the people have heard the gospel but rejected it, or their grandparents accepted a noncontextualized presentation that subsequent generations rejected as culturally inappropriate. Some peoples were once Christian, but they were never taught to understand and propagate the gospel among themselves. When the missionaries left—or were forced to leave—the people reverted to their former religions. If there is even the slightest risk of history repeating itself, missionaries must strive to establish ministries that disciple disciplers, teach teachers and train trainers in order to minimize the danger of creating even more areas of the world that bear the name Christian, but have not been taught all that Christ commanded (Matthew 28:18-20). Why focus on the inadequacies of some missionaries' need for speed in a chapter on the Global South? A glance at much of the church throughout the Global South reveals that such strategies and methods have left swaths of anemic and aberrant Christianity in their wake.

THE SHIFT TO THE GLOBAL SOUTH

The decades since the Industrial Revolution have been dominated by Western powers in virtually every way. That reality is changing. As nations have educated their populations, launched their own industries and in some cases nationalized those once belonging to others, their economies are now forces to be reckoned with. Missiologists should consider these dynamics as well because the wealth of a nation affects such matters as government policies, poverty, crime, immigration patterns and education.

Populations may grow through childbirth or immigration, but when populations grow more quickly than governments and societies anticipate and are prepared to handle, the results are often catastrophic. Surging populations overtax natural resources, government services, waste management, food supplies and police protection. Predicting population growth patterns enables governments and business sectors to anticipate needs and be prepared to meet them. Missiologists must keep a finger on the pulse of growth or decline of the populations as well as concomitant government

planning. It is startling to realize that the world is more often prepared to provide fast food franchises and Internet bandwidth than
the church is to reach, teach and plant churches.

During Teddy Roosevelt's administration, the United States
could "walk softly and carry a big stick," and most nations would
walk with us. Through subsequent decades the United States has
both shortened its stick by weakening its military might and re-
treated from the role of global policeman. This drastic change in US
foreign policy prompted the *Economist* to query, "What would
America fight for?" It called the United States' dramatic shift the
"decline of deterrence."[7]

The sheer numbers of the Global South countries is an advantage for these nations that were formerly considered compara-
tively weak or inconsequential. The numbers they bring to the table
are complemented by huge investments in their war machines with
capital (often derived from petroleum). The United States and other
powerful Western nations are not necessarily their friends as the
case once was. Some Western missionaries are learning that this
influences the citizens of Global South countries, fairly or not. Missionaries may have been welcomed in the past because of their
Western nation citizenship, but that favored position is waning.
Indeed, in some cases it works against missionaries, as is seen in
many Muslim cultures and even in the Americas.[8]

RELIGIOUS REALITIES OF THE GLOBAL SOUTH

Animism is a religious worldview that permeates many Global
South people groups. Animism is based on the belief that everything in the world has a spirit or life force. In addition, there are
benevolent, malevolent and ambivalent spirits as well as spirits of
the recently departed dead, who must be considered daily and
often appeased. What was once considered the primitive
worldview of tribal peoples who embraced an "unevolved" super-

stitious belief system based on magic and old wives tales is finding its way into presidential offices and the boardrooms of the powerful policy shapers.

Regional expressions of most world religions are often blended with animism, and the resulting syncretism—folk religion—is embraced by the general populace. Many adherents do not know how their folk religion and practice differs from the official theology and practice of the world religion they supposedly embrace. International press reports reveal that many people in the Global South believe witchcraft, voodoo, curses, hexes and sorcery are powerfully effective in sports, business, family relations, wealth and politics. When such folk religion is accepted as normative in a society, those who rise to power also embrace this animistic worldview.

Many say that we live in a postmodern world. The premodern world explained the mysteries of nature via ghosts, demons and spirits, and tried to control natural events through curses, spells, powers and the like. Modernity began in the 1600s with the empirical sciences, which sought rational explanations for natural phenomena. This led to advances in technology and medicine among other things. Postmodernism, a movement of the West since the 1950s, is critical of modernism and embraces a multiplicity of explanations for reality. Missionaries should be aware that many of the Global South cultures are not only not postmodern, they are not even modern yet. What Paul Hiebert referred to as the excluded middle of spirits, magic and so on defines virtually all of life.[9]

Worldview is not only how we see and interpret our daily experience, it answers the big questions of life, such as what is real, how we know anything, where we come from and where we go when we die. Everyone views and practices daily life through their worldview. Because a worldview is unseen and is usually subconscious, missionaries in animistic areas must intentionally research what traditional beliefs exist in order to consider their impact on society, especially when negotiating the minefield of culture shock and adaptation.

Islam, Hinduism, Buddhism, Confucianism and Christianity all find homes in the Global South. Just as populations, economies and political powers ebb and flow throughout the world, so do concentrations of these religions. While Islam is traditionally found in nations of the Middle East, Asia and North Africa, it is increasingly common to see burqas, hijabs and abayas in Latin America as well. Middle Eastern nations are flexing their economic muscle and befriending leftist Latin leaders who share distaste for the United States. Mutually beneficial international loans, construction projects and economic development deals are struck, and these are followed by friendlier relations, which encourage immigration.

Just as globalization intersperses the world's populations, the world's religions are spread as well. While exclusivist religions such as Christianity and Islam find little room for other religious beliefs in their codified doctrinal positions, South Asia's Buddhism and Hinduism are more accommodating. While in London in 2013 leading a team to engage immigrant Hindus, Buddhists and Muslims, I and others held frank and friendly conversations with various religious adherents in their temples and mosques. I could not help but wonder about the impact that these numerous immigrants will have on one another's religions, customs and worldviews. Missionaries and Christian workers in London and other major urban centers of the world must take into account the current population reality. They cannot hope to find success in ministering to a caricature of past history. The world seems to have been shaken, and all peoples have been scattered to far-flung locations. Regarding this, missionaries should keep two things in mind: the shaking and scattering is not over, and as peoples relocate they bring their former cultures, worldviews, religions and customs with them.

Cults and health-and-wealth heresies. As I have traveled through the Global South in Africa, Asia and Latin America, I have noticed that the biggest, shiniest, most successful and best-located churches are either cults or heretical versions of Christianity that focus on health-and-wealth. The Mormons have beautiful modern buildings with bronze fixtures, smoked glass, parking lots and sports fields in great locations, all designed so similarly that they could be identified without a sign. The Jehovah's Witnesses have well-located Kingdom Halls for their well-dressed followers. The health-and-wealth heresies are housed in some of the nicest facilities of all. It seemed to me that one of the most prolific of Nigeria's contemporary scourges is the countless health-and-wealth churches.

One of the most successful manifestations of this modern phenomenon is the Universal Church of the Kingdom of God. Some Brazilians in São Paulo recently described it to me as a "business church," explaining that it was a church with teaching about making money. In Spanish-speaking Latin America they call the Universal Church of the Kingdom of God "Pare de Sufrir," which means "Stop suffering." Its doctrine and preaching focuses on having all the money and success you want, with none of the traditional ills. Think Joel Osteen's message on steroids. These kinds of prosperity "gospel" groups are growing exponentially around the world, offering freedom to the oppressed, riches to the poor, health to the sick and hope to the hopeless. The very things that Christ actually offers freely, they offer for a price. David Bledsoe, missionary to Brazil, the birthplace of the Universal Church of the Kingdom of God, conducted extensive investigative research on the group. He reported that members give sacrificially in hopes of receiving promised riches and spiritual covering from satanic attack. When the hoped for riches do not materialize, the fear of satanic attack keeps them in the fold of the church for fear of losing this covering. One Brazilian evangelical explained the cult to me: "They preach deliverance from poverty and oppression, but cause more of both than anyone." Their presentation of themselves as a Christian denomination, as Mormons and Jehovah's Witnesses also do, confuses many. When beliefs of different groups are placed on a continuum, from biblical truth on one end to extremes of heresy on the other, some groups may seem tame by comparison—even resisting the "cult" label—but at the end of the day, how much heresy is harmless?

Pentecostalization. Many mainline denominations, as well as churches planted by fundamentalist independent churches, often take on a more energetic and exuberant worship style in Global South countries. Harvey Cox has written extensively on the Pentecostal movement as well as the Pentecostalization of churches in some regions of the world. While not all Pentecostals stress Oneness doctrine or Jesus only[10]—Pentecostal views of God and soteriology—those who do cannot be embraced as evangelical churches with alternative doctrinal views. This makes the Pentecostalization of mainline and Baptist churches all the more troublesome. What is dubbed "Pentecostal" is sometimes simply an exuberant worship style with clapping and dancing; although it may include running aisles and swooning in worship services. Almost all denominations exhibit more energetic and demonstrative worship forms in the warm cultures of the Global South than is found in the same denominational churches in colder climates of the United States and the United Kingdom.[11] Harvey Cox attributes the desire for this style of worship as the primary reason that the Pentecostalization of these churches is so prevalent, believing that the colder worship forms of Western Christianity left a vacuum.

The dangers of Pentecostalization include requiring signs and wonders or tongues as essential to demonstrate the Spirit's presence and work, emphasizing unquestioning loyalty to the pastor, and subjective hermeneutics ("God told me . . ."). The combination of more vibrant worship expressions, poorly trained pastors and con-

Missiological Implications

Powerful national alliances in the Global South are threatening the relevance of northern nations. Their sheer numbers both tax national resources and provide strength—troop strength during times of war, laborers in the national workforce and family members to care for the aging. While each of these areas requires the government to expend resources, it is compensated in return.

The norms, values, preferences and worldviews of the Global South are identified in advertising, international laws and trade. As these areas become more pervasive, they influence traditional Western thought and practice. The West's individualistic, survival-of-the-fittest mentality is tempered by increased contact with those of a collectivistic, group orientation. Political maneuvering and creative diplomatic truth may seem chaotic, unfair, undemocratic or unethical to dichotomistic thinkers in the traditional West, but nonetheless the holistic approach of Global South cultures is finding expression in business contracts, international law, treaties and even gospel presentations. To be relevant, missionaries must learn the cultural preferences of the Global South and consider how evangelical Christianity may be contextualized therein.

Missionaries must learn how to interact effectively with the gatekeepers of divergent worldviews in the Global South. Religious realities such as animism, which once seemed naive or unenlightened, are now in force and legitimized by ruling classes that embrace such beliefs. This often results in increased syncretism for expediency or societal harmony that cannot be easily challenged or dismissed. Missionaries of the Global South cannot avoid syncretism. We must work to understand the existing worldview and beliefs, and must be ever vigilant against the insidious slide toward an expression of Christianity that is more cultural than Christian.

The Western missionary's role. The role of Western missionaries should be nothing more nor less than what God desires it to be. All the changes and trends throughout the world—those that are happening now as well as those to come—should not be allowed to challenge what God has called his church to do. Though the gospel is unchanging, the task unyielding and the urgency unceasing, the roles we each have to play may indeed change.

Consider the pioneer farmer hacking the life out of a jungle. In the beginning the farmer clears land, burns the vines and scrub bushes, cuts the timber into lumber, builds a home, plows and plants, hoes, and harvests. Then in the next season the farmer plants more strategically, rotates crops to preserve the delicate balance of the soil's nutrients, and brings in animals to assist in farming and to supplement the family diet. Soon he hires others to help bring in more produce from the land, providing responsible work for others. The farmer moves from being a subsistence pioneer to a successful agriculturalist. A pioneer missionary works in the same way, moving from pioneer to one who disciples the saved, plants churches, trains leaders and trainers, and leaves the work in their hands as a fully functioning New Testament community.

As modern missionaries we must constantly examine our role in the global expansion of Christianity. Must Western missionaries always be pioneers? Must they always be preachers? With the changes in world economies, politics, religious realities and come what may, it is time to pause and look at what we hold in our hands, that which we bring to the table. How can we best serve the Lord in our time?

The Western nations are not what they once were, with seemingly unending economic resources and hordes going to the mission fields. Though God is still calling, we do not have the financial resources of previous years. Nevertheless, we are still operating with a missions mindset from the days when finances were more plentiful. Our mission agencies operate much like a formerly prosperous church of two thousand members that strives to fill all the roles and committee structures even though it now has only two hundred members.

But the West never had enough people and funds to reach the world as Jesus commanded in the Great Commission, and it was not supposed to. He did not give the task to the Western church; he gave it to the worldwide church. William Carey understood that. When he arrived on the mission field and saw the overwhelmingly large numbers of Indians, he remarked that if India would ever be won to Christ the Indians would have to do it. This same principle remains true today. Nationals must be trained to fulfill the task, not only because we could never amass enough missionaries to do the task but also in order for everyone to do what God is calling *them* to do.

The mission field has become a mission force. Yet, without proper training and education, zeal for missions is often zeal without knowledge. Missions candidates passionate to reach the world for Christ's sake have sometimes rushed to missions engagement only to fail and return for lack of education, logistical assistance, financial support or intercultural training. All who are called to missions must realize that God is calling people from around the world to this great task and should work to facilitate that reality, each one bringing to the table what God has entrusted to him or her. Since missionaries must increasingly find creative ways to legally enter and reside in many countries of the world, perhaps a key contribution from the West would be to provide training in sound doctrine, missions methods, administration, accounting, logistical support, intercultural skills and knowledge of world religions and worldviews.

A "ridiculous" scenario. Consider the following "ridiculous" scenario. What if one hundred people presented themselves for missionary service this year, and all one hundred felt called to a Global South country that has had evangelical missionaries and believers in their churches for a hundred years? Would it be foolish to send them there? Some would say yes, arguing that the need of the hour is to reach those who have never heard, not to help bring in the harvest. Yet what if the Holy Spirit is planning an awakening and revival there and wants a trained and prepared force in place to bring in and disciple new believers, form them into churches, help them recognize their call and gifting, prepare them for missionary service, and send them to places we cannot go easily or minister crossculturally as well as they can? You may ask how we can know where those places are. We can't. For that reason we must affirm that the Holy Spirit will call people to the mission field as he purposes, and help them get to the places he calls them and do the work he has called them to do.

Reaching & Teaching International Ministries works to train national pastors and leaders around the world. Our motto is "All of God's people going into all the world to obey all of the Great Commission." Toward that end, the ministry's mission is to train trainers and facilitate their involvement in continuing the work in increasing multiplication. Reaching & Teaching began in Ecuador with teachers from the United States and Ecuador. Since then work has begun in the Dominican Republic with primarily Dominican teachers, who subsequently began a Reaching & Teaching training center in Haiti. A corps of international teachers from Peru, Bolivia, Mexico and Colombia soon joined the Dominican and Ecuadorian brothers. Recently the ministry was invited to begin training in the East African countries of Burundi and Rwanda, and extending northward as far as Egypt. The only way that they could embrace such an ambitious project was to agree to come periodically and train trainers in one spot, and they would subsequently fan out into their respective countries to continue the training.

The international team of teachers brings strengths to the ministry. Each teacher adheres to a common confessional statement, which ensures unity on essential doctrines to avoid creating confusion among their students. Yet each brings cultural understandings that are invisible to most Westerners. Their cultural, linguistic and worldview diversity complemented by their life experiences give them insights and depth to teach the same set of truths in ways that are not only culturally appropriate but amazingly effective. God is not only expanding the church throughout the Global South, he is calling men and women to serve in leadership. When they lack training and education, those who have it should provide it. When they are discipled, trained and called, we must lock arms with them and join the work to train up trainers in still more places. All of God's people going into all the world to obey all of the Great Commission.

Conclusion

WHY DID TIME STOP at the point of horses and buggies, straw hats, long-sleeved shirts and overalls for the Amish? Why did some orthodox Jewish hat styles stop with the tall crowned, broad-brimmed felt fedora? Why were these hat and clothing styles embraced but all newer ones were rejected? Why did time freeze with those elements? Do we have similar traditions that should be examined? Things that we continue to do simply because that is the way we have always done them? I think so. I have heard some say that whenever our churches do something new they have to do it right the first time because they are going to be doing it that way for two hundred years.

The Amazon River beckons adventurers and explorers in the same way that Mount Everest attracts mountain climbers. While many have tried to explore the Amazon territory through the centuries, very few have traveled its length, braving the dangers from its Andean beginnings to where it empties into the Atlantic. Tales of the experiences of those who have are fascinating but impossible to repeat. The river rises and rages with annual rains, crashes into and around boulders and logjams, overflows its banks, carves new paths, and leaves behind orphaned oxbow lakes as it changes course.

The massive river system today is similar in many respects to the one that Francisco de Orellana and his men traveled in 1542, but it has also greatly changed. In addition to the new paths that the river cuts, the water flowing through it constantly changes as well. Heraclitus said, "You cannot step into the same river twice." Time changes all things and all people.

Like an ever-rolling river, the world and its cultures and customs also adapt, develop and change continuously. When changes and innovations come, the question before responsible gatekeepers is whether it would be healthy for their community to welcome and incorporate the change, and what the rules of engagement or fair-use guidelines should be. It would be just as foolish for a community to bar and exclude all modern inventions and developments as it would be to fling the door wide open and accept them all without discernment.

While businesses and governments invest massive amounts of money and people to stay abreast of trends that will affect their global reality in both the near and distant future, missionaries have not historically kept pace. Perhaps it seems unspiritual to do so, or even unnecessary since the God of the future is also the God of our mission efforts, and he can lead us where and how he wants. However, the Bible is full of examples of God using human efforts to accomplish his work. Not only is such preparation not unnecessary or unspiritual, the failure to do so is irresponsible. In the jungle at the foot of the mountains, the father of a family near the river takes into account rainstorms he notices at higher elevations and moves his family to higher ground before the flooding begins. Likewise, we must study the trends of change and anticipate global developments to be proactive in missions ministry rather than continue racing from disaster to disaster in reactionary response to changes.

Throughout missions history, each generation has had new questions to answer, or at least variations on older questions that faced their predecessors. But today's greater velocity of change and innovation requires greater vigilance from missions leaders and missionaries regarding embracing and utilizing new technologies. We must never stop wondering, *What's changing, what's new, what's coming tomorrow, and what does it mean for us?* We must be aware of the changes that sweep across the globe with increasing frequency and speed—yes, being vigilant against the threats but also prepared to employ every beneficial innovation for the advance of God's kingdom and the glory of Christ.

The world is changing in complexity, and missionaries must wisely prepare to meet the world that will greet them tomorrow. This will be possible only by approaching their ministries with an open Bible, an open newspaper and an open mind.

A single book cannot hope to consider every change facing our world today; nor can it plumb the depths and exhaust the details of any one of them. My goal has been to point out some peaks on the graph and sensitize us to some of today's realities and developing trends so that missions leaders and missionaries will be prepared for them. My goal is to encourage procedures and policies to help us stay attuned and current so missionaries may engage the world that is and will be rather than the one that was. Each church, mission agency and field missionary should develop a plan and the discipline to stay current, aware, and prepared for today and the world of tomorrow. As uncomfortable as changing how we operate might seem in some quarters, that is not enough—even greater vigilance is required.

There is a more crucial task before the missionary—even more than ensuring appropriate contextualization of the gospel and Christianity, and watching future trends and making changes to appropriately engage the future. The most vital and challenging aspect is to make the essential changes while safeguarding what must never change—the gospel once for all delivered to the saints.

The unchanging reality is that people who have not been reached are lost and must hear the gospel, repent and be born again. Those who have embraced Christ must be discipled to rightly understand and apply God's Word. New disciples must be assembled into New Testament churches with biblically qualified teachers and preachers. The pastors and leaders must be trained. And each church must then continue the process by reaching and teaching others.

In a constantly changing world it is easy to get overwhelmed, dig in and become entrenched where we are, but then we miss the blessing that could be ours. Some are early adopters who embrace every wind that blows and easily forget the things that should never change. The challenge is to embrace the innovations that will facilitate kingdom advance (while passing by the others) and to hold tightly to the unchanging message of the gospel, without which no one can be saved. Great wisdom, diligence, open-mindedness and awareness are essential to lead in effective missions, today and tomorrow. Never forget that in this constantly changing world, we have been given an unchanging commission:

> And Jesus came and said to them, "All authority in heaven and on earth has been given to me. Go therefore and make disciples of all nations, baptizing them in the name of the Father and of the Son and of the Holy Spirit, teaching them to observe all that I have commanded you. And behold, I am with you always, to the end of the age." (Matthew 28:18-20)

Acknowledgments

I HAVE BEEN FORTUNATE TO WRITE SEVERAL BOOKS, and the common theme among them is that they would not have been possible if not for the many individuals who contribute to my life, ministry and writing. It usually begins in my classrooms, since it is through teaching that I often first identify the needs not otherwise covered in published resources. I am always grateful for thoughtful, engaged and inquisitive students who help me to identify the challenges they will face as they step onto the mission field.

In addition to my time in the classroom, I am blessed to have the opportunity to travel around the world, preaching, teaching and consulting with national believers, missionaries and missions agencies. My time with nationals and missionaries always challenges and encourages me. It sharpens my thinking to hear about their ministries and opportunities, and help them think through difficulties they sometimes face. It also helps me to identify some of the specific challenges that have become chapters in this book. I am so grateful to all of those who open their ministries and homes to me as I travel, trusting that through the engagement and conversations we share that the kingdom of God will be strengthened and advanced.

A significant challenge I faced as I have been writing this book is that the ministry I lead, Reaching & Teaching International Ministries, is growing by leaps and bounds. I've always kept a full plate of responsibilities, but this really has been an extraordinarily busy season. I'm so grateful to the entire IVP team, but especially Al Hsu, who has been so helpful throughout the development of this manuscript. Also a great support is Andrew Wolgemuth, who provides additional publishing feedback and guidance so that I'm able to focus as much as possible on ministry while he handles the logistics. During this busy season not only the publishing support but our entire team at Reaching & Teaching International Ministries has helped make this book a reality. Our missionaries, staff and board have all stepped up to do everything necessary to be faithful to what God is doing. They have been courageous, flexible, creative and servant minded. I would not have been able to continue a writing ministry in the midst of such growth if they had not stepped up so remarkably, and I'm deeply grateful. Many have contributed insights, arguments and counsel to guide and improve my thinking as I have grappled with best practices to help missionaries be prepared for contemporary and future realities. However, any remaining errors or weaknesses in the book are my fault.

No acknowledgment that I will ever write would be complete without mention of my incredible family. They cheer me on, make me laugh and bring me incredible joy no matter the task before me. My wife keeps me steady and supported on the days I feel overwhelmed. She makes me laugh and is my best sounding board. My children and their spouses provide constant grounding through inside jokes and reminders of the amazing people they have become. And my grandchildren bring me joy that cannot be paralleled. Seeing the common love we have for the Lord and each other, the ministries that God has given to my wife and children, and the hope of the future in the eyes of my grandchildren encourages me to be the best I can be in all that God gives me. I could not do anything without my family, and I am deeply grateful to them.

Finally and most importantly I am thankful to the Lord for all his goodness to me. He continues to bless my meager efforts and enables me to serve him by his grace and for his glory. He calls me to purity and holiness, forgives me when I fall so short of it, and reminds me of the world's great need for the gospel through the joy, peace and hope I find in my own repenting and returning.

> Now to him who is able to do far more abundantly than all that we ask or think, according to the power at work within us, to him be glory in the church and in Christ Jesus throughout all generations, forever and ever. Amen. (Ephesians 3:20-21)

Notes

Chapter 1: Competing and Conflicting Missions

[1] Anup Shah, "Today, Around 21,000 Children Died Around the World," *Global Issues*, September 24, 2011, www.globalissues.org/article/715/today-21000-children-died-around-the-world.

[2] "Millions Lack Safe Water," *Water.org*, accessed January 5, 2015, http://water.org/water-crisis/water-facts/water.

[3] "Diarrhoea: Why Children Are Still Dying and What Can Be Done," UNICEF and World Health Organization, 2009, p. 5, accessed August 25, 2014, www.unicef.org/health/files/Final_Diarrhoea_Report_October_2009_final.pdf; "Malaria Fact Sheet," UNICEF, accessed August 25, 2014, www.unicef.org/media/files/MALARIAFACTSHEETAFRICA.pdf.

[4] "Global Water, Sanitation, and Hygiene," Center for Disease Control and Prevention, accessed August 25, 2014, www.cdc.gov/healthywater/global.

[5] John Stott, *Christian Mission in the Modern World* (Downers Grove, IL: InterVarsity Press, 2008).

[6] David Hesselgrave, *Paradigms in Conflict: 10 Key Questions in Christian Missions Today* (Grand Rapids: Kregel, 2005), pp. 117-39.

[7] Kevin DeYoung and Greg Gilbert, *What Is the Mission of the Church? Making Sense of Social Justice, Shalom and the Great Commission* (Wheaton, IL: Crossway, 2011).

[8] John Piper, *Let the Nations Be Glad! The Supremacy of God in Missions*, 3rd ed. (Grand Rapids: Baker Academic, 2010), p. 15.

[9] Brother Yun, Peter Xu Yongze, Enoch Wang and Paul Hattaway, *Back to Jerusalem: Three Chinese House Church Leaders Share Their Vision to Complete the Great Commission* (Downers Grove, IL: InterVarsity Press, 2005).

Chapter 2: Urbanization and Globalization

[1] "Urbanization," United Nations, accessed January 5, 2015, www.un.org

/en/development/desa/population/theme/urbanization.

[2]"World Urbanization Prospects: The 2011 Revision," United Nations Department of Economic and Social Affairs/Population Division, March 2012, p. 1, http://ipcc-wg2.gov/njlite_download2.php?id=8085.

[3]Neal Lineback and Mandy Lineback Gritzner, "Geography in the News: The Growth of Megacities," *National Geographic*, February 17, 2014, http://news watch.nationalgeographic.com/2014/02/17/geography-in-the-news-the -growth-of-megacities.

[4]Joel Kotkin and Wendell Cox, "The World's Fastest-Growing Megacities," *Forbes*, April 8, 2013, www.forbes.com/sites/joelkotkin/2013/04/08/the -worlds-fastest-growing-megacities.

[5]"The Twenty Most Populous Countries in 1950, 1999 and 2050," United Nations, accessed January 6, 2015, www.un.org/esa/population/pubs archive/india/20most.htm.

[6]"Globalization," World Health Organization, accessed January 6, 2015, www.who.int/trade/glossary/story043/en.

[7]Chiamaka Nwosu, Jeanne Batalova and Gregory Auclair, "Frequently Requested Statistics on Immigrants and Immigration in the United States," Migration Policy Institute, April 28, 2014, www.migrationpolicy.org /article/frequently-requested-statistics-immigrants-and-immigration -united-states-2.

[8]Rebecca Evans, "Muhammad Becomes London's Favourite Boy's Name but Harry Still Comes Out Top Overall," *Daily Mail*, August 12, 2013, www.dailymail.co.uk/news/article-2390945/Muhammad-Londons -favourite-boys-Harry-comes-overall.html.

[9]Nwosu, Batalova and Auclair, "Frequently Requested Statistics."

[10]Ralph D. Winter and Bruce A. Koch, "Finishing the Task: The Unreached Peoples Challenge," *International Journal of Frontier Missions* 19, no. 4 (Winter 2002): 18, www.ijfm.org/PDFs_IJFM/19_4_PDFs/winter_koch _task.pdf.

[11]Dr. Orville Boyd Jenkins, "What Is a People Group?," International Mission Board, http://public.imb.org/globalresearch/Pages/PeopleGroup.aspx.

[12]"Definitions: People Group," Joshua Project, accessed January 6, 2015, http://joshuaproject.net/help/definitions.

[13]Karen R. Humes, Nicholas A. Jones and Roberto R. Ramirez, "Overview of Race and Hispanic Origin: 2010," U.S. Census Bureau, March 2011, p. 2, www.census.gov/prod/cen2010/briefs/c2010br-02.pdf.

[14]Edward Retta and Cynthia Brink, "Latino or Hispanic Panic: Which Term Should We Use?," *Cross-Culture Communications*, 2007, www.cross culturecommunications.com/latino-hispanic.pdf.

[15]"To keep pace with rapidly changing notions of race, the Census Bureau wants to make broad changes to its surveys that would treat 'Hispanic' as a distinct category regardless of race, end use of the term 'Negro' and offer new ways to identify Middle Easterners.

"For instance, because Hispanic is currently defined as an ethnicity and not a race, some 18 million Latinos—or roughly 37 percent—used the 'some other race' category on their census forms to establish a Hispanic racial identity." Hope Yen, "Census Seeks Changes in How It Measures Race," *Associated Press*, August 8, 2012, http://bigstory.ap.org/article /census-seeks-changes-how-it-measures-race.

[16]Jens Manuel Krogstad and D'Vera Cohn, "U.S. Census Looking at Big Changes in How It Asks About Race and Ethnicity," *Pew Research Center*, March 14, 2014, www.pewresearch.org/fact-tank/2014/03/14/u-s-census -looking-at-big-changes-in-how-it-asks-about-race-and-ethnicity.

[17]Dave Nodar, "What Are Characteristics of the New Evangelization?," *ChristLife*, 2000, www.christlife.org/evangelization/articles/C_newevan .html.

[18]Kevin Cotter, "What Is the New Evangelization?," *Catholic Exchange*, June 13, 2013, http://catholicexchange.com/what-is-the-new-evangelization.

CHAPTER 3: TRAVEL, COMMUNICATION AND THE MISSIONARY LIFE

[1]Sherwood G. Lingenfelter and Marvin K. Mayers, *Ministering Cross-Culturally* (Grand Rapids: Baker Academic, 2003), p. 24.

[2]Eugene Burdick and William J. Lederer, *The Ugly American* (London: W. W. Norton, 1958).

[3]Indeed, a recent controversy in Turkey surrounded the fact that their prime minister used such technology for a speech. See Braden Goyette, "Turkish Prime Minister Gives Speech as Giant Hologram," *Huffington Post*, January 28, 2014, www.huffingtonpost.com/2014/01/28/turkish -prime-minister-hologram_n_4680933.html?hpt=hp_bn17.

CHAPTER 4: SHORT-TERM MISSIONS

[1]Robert J. Priest, *Effective Engagement in Short-Term Missions* (Pasadena, CA: William Carey Library, 2012); Robert J. Priest, Terry Dischinger,

Steve Rasmussen and C. M. Brown, "Researching the Short-Term Mission Movement," *Missiology* 34, no. 4 (October 2006): 432.

[2]Ralph D. Winter, "The Re-Amateurization of Missions," *EMS Bulletin*, Spring 1996.

[3]Helpful resources to provide orientation to understanding and working among other cultures are Sarah A. Lanier, *Foreign to Familiar* (Hagerstown, MD: McDougal, 2000); Sherwood G. Lingenfelter and Marvin K. Mayers, *Ministering Cross-Culturally*, 2nd ed. (Grand Rapids: Baker Academic, 2003); and my *Reaching and Teaching the Highland Quichuas* (Wheaton, IL: Reaching & Teaching, 2012).

[4]For more information on this ministry, you can see our website, Reaching & Teaching, at www.reachingandteaching.org.

Chapter 5: Reaching Oral Learners

[1]For a basic introduction to the world of orality, check out Avery Willis and Steve Evans, comps., *Making Disciples of Oral Learners* (Lima, NY: International Orality Network, 2007); Daniel Sheard, *An Orality Primer for Missionaries* (self-published 2007); and M. David Sills, *Reaching and Teaching: A Call to Great Commission Obedience* (Chicago: Moody Publishers, 2010), chap. 9.

[2]Durk Meijer, "How Shall They Hear," presentation at International Orality Network meeting, February 2008.

[3]"Adult and Youth Literacy," UNESCO Institute for Statistics, September 2013, www.uis.unesco.org/literacy/Documents/fs26-2013-literacy-en.pdf.

[4]"Is Your Audience Understanding Your Message," GMI, accessed January 6, 2015, www.gmi.org/infographics/missiographic-Literacy.pdf.

[5]Ibid.

[6]"Literacy Levels," Literacy Cooperative, accessed January 6, 2015, http://literacycooperative.org/litlevels.htm.

[7]James B. Slack, "The Ways People Learn: Exploring the Implications of Orality, Literacy and Chronological Bible Storying Concerning Global Evangelization," IMB Resource Center, http://media1.imbresources.org/files/83/8361/8361-46134.pdf.

[8]A syllogism, for instance, is: If A equals B, and B equals C, then A equals C.

[9]Walter J. Ong, *Orality and Literacy*, 2nd ed. (New York: Routledge, 2002), p. 6.

[10]Herbert V. Klem, *Oral Communication of the Scripture* (Pasadena, CA: William Carey Library, 1981), p. xvii.

[11]MOOC is the acronym for "massive online open course." This model allows hundreds or thousands of students to enroll in the same online course.

Chapter 6: Helping Without Hurting

[1]"Millions Lack Safe Water," Water.org, accessed January 5, 2015, http://water.org/water-crisis/water-facts/water; "Hunger Facts," World Vision, accessed January 6, 2015, http://30hourfamine.org/hunger-facts; "Poverty Overview," World Bank, accessed January 6, 2015, www.worldbank.org/en/topic/poverty/overview.

[2]"10 Facts on Malaria," World Health Organization, updated April 2015, www.who.int/features/factfiles/malaria/en.

[3]"Facts and Figures of a Global Crisis," Global Road Safety Partnership, http://www.grsproadsafety.org/our-knowledge/facts-and-figures-global-crisis.

[4]"11 Facts About Human Trafficking," DoSomething.org, accessed January 6, 2015, www.dosomething.org/facts/11-facts-about-human-trafficking.

[5]Rob Wile, "The Global 20: Twenty Huge Trends That Will Define the World for Decades," *Business Insider*, January 17, 2014, www.businessinsider.com/business-insider-global-20-2014-2014-1.

[6]Justin Gillis, "A Jolt to Complacency on Food Supply," *New York Times*, November 11, 2013, www.nytimes.com/2013/11/12/science/earth/warning-on-global-food-supply.html.

[7]For additional resources on this challenge, see Steve Corbett and Brian Fikkert, *When Helping Hurts* (Chicago: Moody, 2009); and Bob Lupton, *Toxic Charity* (San Francisco: HarperOne, 2012).

[8]Rakesh Kochhar, "10 Projections for the Global Population in 2050," Pew Research Center, February 3, 2014, www.pewresearch.org/fact-tank/2014/02/03/10-projections-for-the-global-population-in-2050.

[9]For more on Hiebert's model of critical contextualization, see his *Anthropological Reflections on Missiological Issues* (Grand Rapids: Baker, 1994).

[10]The "Three-Self Model" was pioneered more than a century ago by missionaries Henry Venn and Rufus Anderson for developing church plants.

Chapter 7: Churches as Sending Agencies

[1]For additional discussion on this view see my book, *Reaching and Teaching: A Call to Great Commission Obedience* (Chicago: Moody Publishers, 2010), pp. 121-22.

CHAPTER 8: BUSINESS AS MISSION

[1]Business as mission definitions from some contemporary authors: Neal Johnson: "A for-profit commercial business venture that is Christian led, intentionally devoted to being used as an instrument of God's mission to the world (missio dei), and is operated in a cross-cultural environment, either domestic or international." Mats Tunehag: "Business as Mission is about real, viable, sustainable and profitable businesses; with a Kingdom of God purpose, perspective and impact; leading to transformation of people and societies spiritually, economically and socially—to the greater glory of God." Ken Eldred: "Kingdom Businesses [BAMs] are for-profit commercial enterprises in the mission field of the developing world through which Christian business professionals are seeking to meet spiritual, social and economic needs." Rundle and Steffen: "A Great Commission Company is a socially responsible, income-producing business managed by kingdom professionals and created for the specific purpose of glorifying God and promoting the growth and multiplication of local churches in the least-evangelised and least-developed part of the world." Advanced Team Concepts blog, www.atctraining.com/log/2010_05 _advanced_team_concepts_-_blogs_business_as_missions_--_bam _blog.htm.

[2]Richard Reichert, *Daybreak Over Ecuador* (Sandy, UT: Sunrise Press, 1999), p. 50.

[3]"Brother Andrew—God's Smuggler," Friends of the Gospel, http://friendsofthegospel.org/index.php?option=com_content&view=article&id=69&Itemid=84.

[4]Jerry Rankin, "Marketplace Missionaries," *TheRankinFile.com*, June 14, 2012, http://therankinfile.com/2012/06/marketplace-missionaries.

[5]Patrick Lai, *Tentmaking* (Downers Grove, IL: InterVarsity Press, 2006).

[6]Jack Welch, quoted in Scott Allison, "The Responsive Organization," *Forbes*, February 10, 2014, www.forbes.com/sites/scottallison/2014/02/10/the-responsive-organization-how-to-cope-with-technology-and-disruption.

[7]This Chinese missions effort describes itself as the largest missions mobilization movement in history.

[8]Some may doubt this with the low gas prices seen in early 2015 and shale oil being developed. However, some people in the industry say higher

prices will be back. "Former Oil Exec: $5-a-Gallon Gas on the Way," *USA Today,* http://www.usatoday.com/story/money/2015/01/19/gas-oil-five-dollar-gallon/21865975/.

[9]Matt Ridley, "The Scarcity Fallacy," *Wall Street Journal,* April 26-27, 2014, C1-C2.

[10]Ernesto Sirolli, "Want to Help Someone? Shut Up and Listen," TED, September 2012, www.ted.com/talks/ernesto_sirolli_want_to_help_someone_shut_up_and_listen?utm_campaign=&utm_source=direct-on.ted.com&utm_medium=on.ted.com-static&utm_content=awesm-publisher&awesm=on.ted.com_Sirolli.

CHAPTER 9: CHANGING GOVERNMENTS

[1]The premise of this chapter was further illustrated as edits were being completed on this chapter and President Obama announced significant changes to the relationship between the United States and Cuba. It is not likely that we will know the implications of this change before this book goes to print, but the reality that the information in the chapter on changing governments is not consistent long enough for the book to get to print is indicative of the challenge facing us today.

[2]"The Foundation for Haiti's Recovery," *UNCCD News* 2, no. 1 (January-February 2010), http://newsbox.unccd.int/2.1/img/UNCCDNews2,1LR72a.pdf.

[3]"Latin America's Political Outlook in the Wake of the Current Election Cycle," Brookings, October 14, 2014, www.brookings.edu/events/2014/10/14-latin-america-political-outlook.

[4]Rob Wile, "The Global 20: Twenty Huge Trends That Will Define the World for Decades," *Business Insider,* January 17, 2014, www.businessinsider.com/business-insider-global-20-2014-2014-1?tru=JMknL#1-the-bric-era-is-over.

[5]Tom Phillips, "China on Course to Become 'World's Most Christian Nation' Within 15 Years," *Telegraph,* April 19, 2014, www.telegraph.co.uk/news/worldnews/asia/china/10776023/China-on-course-to-become-worlds-most-Christian-nation-within-15-years.html.

[6]Matthew Miller, "China's 'Ordinary' Billionaire Behind Grand Nicaragua Canal Plan," Reuters, May 4, 2014, www.reuters.com/article/2014/05/04/us-china-canal-insight-idUSBREA4309E20140504.

[7]Ibid.

[8]Nicolas van de Walle, review of *China's Second Continent: How a Million Migrants Are Building a New Empire in Africa,* by Howard W. French, *Foreign Affairs,* November-December 2014, www.foreignaffairs.com /reviews/capsule-review/china-s-second-continent-how-a-million -migrants-are-building-new-empire-africa.

[9]Jean-Pierre Lehmann, "China's Leader Xi Jinping Takes Global Center Stage," *Forbes,* November 30, 2014, www.forbes.com/sites/jplehmann/2014 /11/30/chinas-leader-xi-jinping-takes-global-center-stage.

[10]Farouk Chothia, "Who Are Nigeria's Boko Haram Islamists?," BBC News, January 21, 2015, www.bbc.com/news/world-africa-13809501.

[11]"Arab Spring," *Oxford Dictionaries,* accessed January 14, 2015, www .oxforddictionaries.com/us/definition/american_english/Arab-Spring.

[12]Patrick Cockburn, "Who Are Isis? The Rise of the Islamic State in Iraq and the Levant," *The Independent,* April 21, 2015, www.independent .co.uk/news/world/middle-east/who-are-isis-the-rise-of-the-islamic -state-in-iraq-and-the-levant-9541421.html.

[13]Alessandria Masi, "Where to Find ISIS Supporters," *International Business Times,* October 9, 2014, www.ibtimes.com/where-find-isis-supporters -map-militant-groups-aligned-islamic-state-group-1701878; "ISIL claims massacre of Ethiopian Christians in Libya," Al Jazeera, April 20, 2015, www.aljazeera.com/news/middleeast/2015/04/isil-claims-massacre -ethiopian-christians-libya-150419104309814.html.

[14]Eliott C. McLaughlin, "ISIS Executes More Christians in Libya, Video Shows," CNN, April 20, 2015, www.cnn.com/2015/04/19/africa/libya-isis -executions-ethiopian-christians/index.html.

[15]Susie Steiner, "Sharia Law," *Guardian,* August 20, 2002, www .theguardian.com/world/2002/aug/20/qanda.islam.

[16]Ibid.

[17]Ibid.

[18]Lionel Beehner, "Religious Conversion and Sharia Law," Council on Foreign Relations, June 8, 2007, www.cfr.org/malaysia/religious -conversion-sharia-law/p13552.

[19]"Libya Assembly Votes for Sharia Law," Al Jazeera, December 4, 2013, www.aljazeera.com/news/africa/2013/12/libya-assembly-votes-sharia -law-201312415321760343.html.

[20]Ankit Panda, "Brunei Becomes First East Asian State to Adopt Sharia Law," *Diplomat,* October 25, 2013, http://thediplomat.com/2013/10

/brunei-becomes-first-east-asian-state-to-adopt-sharia-law.

[21]Omar Sacirbey, "Sharia Law in the USA 101," *Huffington Post*, July 29, 2013, www.huffingtonpost.com/2013/07/29/sharia-law-usa-states-ban _n_3660813.html.

[22]"Christian Persecution," Open Doors, www.opendoorsusa.org/Christian -persecution.

[23]"The American Embassy Warden System is a communication cascade that allows Americans to receive security warnings and other important notices as quickly as possible. Wardens are resident American citizens who volunteer to contact other Americans in their area or organization with important information from the Embassy or the Department of State." "Warden Information," US Embassy, Kinshasa, Congo, accessed January 14, 2015, http://kinshasa.usembassy.gov /wardensystem3.html.

CHAPTER 10: THE GLOBAL SOUTH, SOUTHERN CHURCH AND ROLE OF WESTERN MISSIONARIES

[1]Todd M. Johnson, "Christianity in Global Context: Trends and Statistics," Pew Forum on Religion and Public Life, accessed January 16, 2015, www.pewforum.org/uploadedfiles/Topics/Issues/Politics_and_Elections /051805-global-christianity.pdf.

[2]"American People's Affinity Group," PowerPoint presentation by Marty and Melissa Childers, Affinity Connection Strategists, International Mission Board, Southern Baptist Convention, 2010.

[3]For greater detail on the history of the unreached–reached designation, originator's intent and contemporary application, see M. David Sills, *Reaching and Teaching: A Call to Great Commission Obedience* (Chicago: Moody Publishers, 2010).

[4]"World Urbanization Prospects Highlights: The 2014 Revision," United Nations Department of Economic and Social Affairs, 2014, http://esa .un.org/unpd/wup/Highlights/WUP2014-Highlights.pdf.

[5]Ibid.

[6]Indeed, this is already true if you embrace the belief that reached people groups are those that are 2 percent or more evangelical.

[7]"What Would America Fight For?," *Economist*, May 3, 2014; "The Decline of Deterrence," *Economist*, May 3, 2014.

[8]Deann Alford, "Venezuela to Expel New Tribes Mission," *Christianity*

Today, October 14, 2005, www.christianitytoday.com/ct/2005/octoberweb-only/53.0a.html.

[9]For more information see Paul G. Hiebert, *Transforming Worldviews* (Grand Rapids: Baker Academic, 2008), and *Anthropological Reflections on Missiological Issues* (Grand Rapids: Baker Academic, 1994).

[10]Oneness Pentecostal theology affirms that there exists only one God in the universe. It affirms the deity of Jesus and the Holy Spirit. However, Oneness theology denies the Trinity. The Trinity is the doctrine that there is one God who manifests himself as three distinct, simultaneous persons. The Trinity does not assert that there are three gods but only one. This is important because many groups who oppose orthodoxy will accuse Trinitarians of believing in three gods. But this is not so. The doctrine of the Trinity is that there is one God in three persons.

Oneness theology denies the Trinity and teaches that God is a single person who was "manifested as Father in creation and as the Father of the Son, in the Son for our redemption, and as the Holy Spirit in our regeneration" (www.upci.org/about/index.asp). Another way of looking at it is that "God revealed himself as Father in the Old Testament, as the Son in Jesus during Christ's ministry on earth, and now as the Holy Spirit after Christ's ascension" (https://carm.org/oneness-pentecostal-theology#footnote1_y5cgk7e).

[11]For more detail on warm cultures see Sarah A. Lanier, *Foreign to Familiar* (Hagerstown, MD: McDougal, 2000).

Recommended Reading

Adeney, Miriam. *Kingdom Without Borders: The Untold Story of Global Christianity*. Downers Grove, IL: InterVarsity Press, 2009.

Corbett, Steve, and Brian Fikkert. *When Helping Hurts: How to Alleviate Poverty Without Hurting the Poor . . . and Yourself*. Chicago: Moody Publishers, 2012.

Detweiler, Craig. *iGods: How Technology Shapes Our Spiritual and Social Lives*. Grand Rapids: Brazos, 2013.

Engel, James F., and William A. Dyrness. *Changing the Mind of Missions: Where Have We Gone Wrong?* Downers Grove, IL: InterVarsity Press, 2000.

Escobar, Samuel. *The New Global Mission: The Gospel from Everywhere to Everyone*. Christian Doctrine in Global Perspective. Downers Grove, IL: InterVarsity Press, 2003.

Friedman, George. *The Next Decade: Where We've Been . . . and Where We're Going*. New York: Random House, 2012.

Hesselgrave, David J. *Paradigms in Conflict: 10 Key Questions in Christian Missions Today*. Grand Rapids: Kregel, 2006.

Hiebert, Paul G. *Anthropological Reflections on Missiological Issues*. Grand Rapids: Baker Academic, 1994.

———. *Transforming Worldviews: An Anthropological Understanding of How People Change*. Grand Rapids: Baker Academic, 2008.

Hiebert, Paul G., R. Daniel Shaw and Tite Tiénou. *Understanding Folk Religion: A Christian Response to Popular Beliefs and Practices*. Grand Rapids: Baker Academic, 1999.

Jenkins, Philip. *The New Faces of Christianity: Believing the Bible in the Global South*. New York: Oxford University Press, 2006.

Jenkins, Philip, and Helen B. Mules. *The Next Christendom: The Coming of Global Christianity*. New York: Oxford University Press, 2003.

Johnstone, Patrick J. *The Future of the Global Church: History, Trends and Possibilities*. Downers Grove, IL: InterVarsity Press, 2011.

Lai, Patrick. *Tentmaking: Business as Missions*. Milton Keynes, UK: Authentic Media, 2005.

Lingenfelter, Sherwood G., Marvin Keene Mayers and Marvin K. Mayers. *Ministering Cross-Culturally: An Incarnational Model for Personal Relationships*. Grand Rapids: Baker, 2003.

Lupton, Robert D. *Toxic Charity: How the Church Hurts Those They Help and How to Reverse It*. San Francisco: HarperOne, 2012.

McQuilkin, Robertson. *The Great Omission*. Grand Rapids: Baker, 1984.

Payne, J. D., *Pressure Points: Twelve Global Issues Shaping the Face of the Church*. Nashville, TN: Thomas Nelson, 2013.

Pocock, Michael, Gailyn Van Rheenen and Douglas McConnell. *The Changing Face of World Missions: Engaging Contemporary Issues and Trends*. Encountering Missions. Grand Rapids: Baker Academic, 2005.

Sills, M. David. *The Missionary Call: Find Your Place in God's Plan for the World*. Chicago: Moody Publishers, 2008.

———. *Reaching and Teaching. A Call to Great Commission Obedience*. Chicago: Moody Publishers, 2010.

Stott, John R. W. *Christian Mission in the Modern World*. Downers Grove, IL: InterVarsity Press, 1975.

Tennent, Timothy C. *Theology in the Context of World Christianity: How the Global Church Is Influencing the Way We Think About and Discuss Theology*. Grand Rapids: Zondervan, 2007.

Wright, Christopher J. H. *The Mission of God: Unlocking the Bible's Grand Narrative*. Downers Grove, IL: IVP Academic, 2006.

About the Author

D R. DAVID SILLS is the founder and president of Reaching & Teaching International Ministries as well as a missions professor at Southern Baptist Theological Seminary. David joined the faculty of Southern Seminary after serving as a missionary in Ecuador. While with the International Mission Board, he served as a church planter and general evangelist among the Highland Quichua people in the Andes and as rector and professor at the Ecuadorian Baptist Theological Seminary. In addition to leadership training and seminary ministry that has taken him throughout Latin America and around the world, David has started and pastored churches in the United States and Ecuador.

David has written several books and articles. His English language books include *The Missionary Call: Find Your Place in God's Plan for the World*, *Reaching and Teaching: A Call to Great Commission Obedience* and *Reaching and Teaching the Highland Quichuas*. *The Missionary Call* has been translated into Spanish, Korean and Indonesian, and he has also written two books in Spanish, *Capacitación Cultural en la Cultura Quichua* and *Quichuas de la Sierra: Descubriendo un Modelo de Adiestramiento Pastoral Culturalmente Apropriado*. In addition, he has also coauthored or served as a contributor on several books, including *Introduction to Global Missions* and *Introducción a la Misiología*.

His unique combination of hands-on field experience, missions leadership, academic contribution and publishing gives David a unique perspective, which he brings to speaking engagements and conferences around the world. As such, he is a frequent conference speaker for national and international missions and ministry conferences. He has previously spoken for the Desiring God National Conference, Urbana Missions Conference, To Every Tribe, Master's College and the Cross Conference among many others.

David and his wife, Mary, have been married for over thirty years and have two married children and several grandchildren. David and Mary's children are all graduates of Southern Baptist Theological Seminary.

Learn more about David and his ministry, Reaching & Teaching International Ministries, at www.reachingandteaching.org.

Name and Subject Index

Scripture Index